WORDS

OF

WEED

AND

WISDOM

By

**Alun Buffry, Clara O'Donnell, Jacqui Malkin,
Jezza Austin, Mars Bilters, Melissa Doordaughter,
Phil Monk, Rocky van de Benderskum, Ryan Kief,
Sarah Dougan and Steve Cook.**

Words of Weed and Wisdom
by
Alun Buffry, Clara O'Donnell, Jacqui Malkin, Jezza Austin, Mars Bilters, Melissa Doordaughter, Phil Monk, Rocky van de Benderskum, Ryan Kief, Sarah Dougan and Steve Cook.

Published by ABeFree Publishing
ISBN 9781916310766

Thanks to ABeFree Publishing for formatting the soft-back edition.
http://www.buffry.org.uk/abefreepublishing.html
ABeFreePublishing@yahoo.com

Cover artwork by Rocky van de Benderskum
Cover design by Alun Buffry using KDP Cover Creator

CONTENTS

FUEL · PAPER · FIBRE · FOOD · MEDICINE
EDUCATE YOURSELF

Tetrahydrocannabinol

CH₃

OH

H

H

H₃C

H₃C

O

C₅H₁₁

WORDS

BY

CLARA O'DONNELL

Clara O'Donnell is a married mum; her daughter was born deaf. Clara has been published in local and national news, Sidewalk Skateboard Magazine, Weed World Magazine, and Limping Chicken, the largest deaf forum in the UK. She also writes a blog. Clara is a qualified Master Herbalist and a Member of the Complimentary Medicine Association In her spare time she raises funds for a village in Cambodia and puts on events in her village to bring the community together. Clara says: "If you want peace in the world, start with your neighbours."

THE WAITING ROOM

Welcome to the waiting room,
It'll be time for you to depart Real soon,
We can't tell you what time or what day,
But you can be sure you are on your way.

Eat what you like, we will cook it for you
Fish and chips or a hearty fresh stew
Here is your garden
It comes with a view

Decorate your room however you like
Bring pictures and balloons and a fairy light
Have your home comforts your favourite clothes
Why people save stuff for best, nobody knows

Feel safe and comforted in your room
You're preventing your family the gloom
Of you dying at home in your own bed
The thought of someone finding you is what you
dread.

So here you are in this little waiting room
Others go faster, it seems so soon
Feeling bad that you can say your goodbyes
When others never do and are left with the whys

Grateful to have these last moments and talk
Thinking about the final walk
When you throw all your glitter and start anew
There's another adventure it's waiting for you

So stop please stop fighting it is okay
There's nothing to do now, nothing to say
You've showered the love and made memories
You've written your letters, there's piles of these.

You keep hanging on in case there's been a mistake
We got it all wrong, Is it ever too late
You can let go, and be on your way
And know that everyone is okay

The tickets are ready they don't show a time
I guess, your guess is as good as mine
The tears that fall are full of sadness
This just seems like utter madness

I admit I do not want to wave you goodbye
The thought just makes me want to cry
So whilst you're waiting I will wait too
I wish there was more I could do for you.

It's so beautiful though this half way place
Full of love and reality and grace
Full of smiles and full of laughs
To help you on your final path.

THE DEPARTURE

Time to say goodbye
No tears. Don't cry
I'm out of pain I feel free
So now say goodbye to me

I'm ready now, I did what I could
If I could have done more, I would
But I've had enough of this fight
It's time to dim my light

When I first knew my time was up
I fought I didn't want to give it up
But these last weeks, I've made my peace
I did what I could before my release

There's things I didn't get to do,
Things I didn't get to say,
I wish I'd had more time, it's true
But it's time to say goodbye to you

No tears please, just love your life
Do it all and don't think twice
I'm out of pain, I'm on my way
Gone tomorrow if not today

My heart is full of all your love
That comes with me sure enough
And though I know your hearts will ache
I am okay I'm out of pain

I'm that glitter that you've never seen
I'm the leaf on your windscreen
I'm the Robin watching you
I'm everywhere, you know it's true

I'll see you on the other side
No need to rush no need to cry
Remember me and don't forget
To Live your life without regret

I'm going now, I don't want to
But I'm ready and you'll get through
Celebrate our times together
Love has no bounds, it is forever.

The waiting room has been fun
But now I really have to run
The tickets ready the time is now
So I will take my final bow.

BABY BABY LITTLE BABY

Baby Baby little Baby
It's time to come from that warm belly.

Your mummy and daddy have waited so long
To sing you a sweet goodnight lullaby song.

The whole world is waiting to say high...
So come on out sweetie-pie.

And try your best not to hurt mummy
When you are descending from her tummy.

Come on baby come this week
To stop the doctors taking a "peek".

Your mummy and daddy will give you hugs
And warm snuggles and lots of love.

XX

NOW YOU ARE SIX

What happened to that silent baby?
The one who would never speak, write or read?
I think perhaps that maybe
They diagnosed you at break neck speed

Those moments when we were threatened
And told we did not have your best interests at heart,
They knew best, I think they reckoned
And how they could have torn our family apart.

I could be mad and angry
I could get out and fight
Because all those LIES they told me
That just cannot be right?

You have a tiny baby
And they will never learn to read,
Although if you are lucky maybe
We can give her an op if you agree.

If you do not get on this train
We can take your rights away
And you will be the blame
Of your daughters silent day.

And then we learnt some sign
And you told me what you need
And suddenly I am fine
As I give you another feed.

And you tell me you want hugs
And you tell me you want kisses
With those tiny toddler hands
You talk and tell me all your wishes

Then one morning as I sleep,
I am woken by a sound.
It says ma ma ma ma,
And I cannot help but look around.

It's you, my silent baby.
You have learned to find your voice
and although I probably shouldn't
I cannot help but feel rejoice.

And now you are six years old
And you love Harry Styles,
You are funny, brave and bold
And you are always full of smiles.

I am constantly projecting on
How your life will be.
Is there anything that I did wrong?
Will you be angry at me?

But I have tried by very best
And I have left you with free choice
And I wouldn't love you any less
If you had never found your voice.

THE SMELL OF FRESHLY CUT GRASS

The smell of freshly cut grass
And bluebells and spring flowers,
The stillness of the trees,
The birds floating in the sky,
No cars, or trucks go by,
Just a bumble bee and a butterfly.

The sun is warm on your face
And your skin and your hair,
One person walks past and smiles,
The clouds are non existent

The sky is blue, and bright.
The river is flowing over pebbles
And looks fresh and inviting.
You take of your shoes,

And walk barefoot
And dip your feet into the water.
It feels so refreshing.
You are at one with nature.

Traffic jam, again, horns beeping,
Angry faces, bored faces lots of faces,
Pass you by as you try
And get to work on time.

You arrive flustered and apologise
And jump to your roll
All day as the sun shines you work,
Thinking, about holidays
And weekends off and friends,

At lunchtime you are too busy
To go out for a break, you eat
As you work at your desk,
Answering the phone between eating

You try and hit deadlines
But doing a favour for your colleague
Has put you behind, the boss looks at his watch.
"Who can stay late?"
You raise your hand whilst inside

Your head is saying, but I promised the kids
Their favourite tea and a story before bed
But you know that wont wash
With the serious boss.

You leave work, straight into gridlock
And sit listening to the news on the radio
War, death, and politics fills your ears.
You stop at a shop
And treat yourself to a bottle of wine.

You get home and kiss your sleeping kids,
Say hello to your partner,
Eat, drink watch a programme on TV
And go to bed, set the alarm
And sleep, and repeat

WHERE DID YOU GO?

Where did you go?
One moment we are chatting about life
And then you are gone
No more calls or texts
No more sofa surfing or bedside talks
There's a space where you were
But there's no sign of you
Sometimes I think I can feel you're there
But I can't see you or hear you
You are just the air everywhere
I waited for a sign but you must be busy
That's what we imagine anyway
I wonder if you've met the others
That left before of after you Is there a connection of
souls
Or are you busy knitting clouds?
Or mixing rainbows or shining up stars
Are you watching over us?
Doing that stuff, fixing things?
Or polishing your angel wings?
I know you know we miss you
I know you see us cry we know you never wanted that
But it's a promise hard to keep
We weep we cry we try not to
But we do, and we are sorry for that
Making memories in your honour
Living out dreams we wanted you to make
Trying hard not to ache
You are out of sight except in dreamland
Where you smile and say its
OK My brave unselfish warrior with wings.
We love you.

AM I ON A DIFFERENT PLANET?

Am I on a different planet?
Than those people who are wrong?
All these angry people shouting
Whilst I sing my peaceful song.

Why can't we all be kind
And look after each other,
Every woman a sister,
Every man a brother?

We all share the same DNA.
We all have the same ancestor mum.
Some of us know our family,
Some of us know none.

And these people in power
Ask us for our votes.
They may as well ask us
If we prefer cows or goats.

There's enough money on the planet
To house, feed and clothe us all
Yet people live on cardboard
As you are shopping at the mall.

People eating out of bins
Or maybe a food bank
People sleeping on the streets
21st century wank.

People shamed for being unable,
People shamed for being gay
Why are we all so fucking judging?
Can't we think before we say?

Do we really hate people so much
That we torment them on the net?
I guess it's easier without a face,
You don't need to feel regret.

All this spite and anger boils me.
Where is compassion, care and kind?
Are we all so busy fighting?
We forgot the word mankind.

MY MAM'S GOT MS

My mam's got MS
And she got arrested
For growing a plant
Because someone protested.

They changed the law
For people like her to be well
But there is no prescriptions
So the police put her in a cell.

They came to her home,
Treated it like a crime scene,
Arrested her and took her away.
This feels like a bad dream.

Meanwhile Britain is one of the greats.
It grows cannabis to send to the United States.
The biggest exporter of medical weed
But not for their own people most in need.

In Britain instead,
In a hospital bed a little boy has fits
But instead of giving him oil to make the boy better
They make him suffer. It's the pits

It's hard to believe that this is the law.
Punish the sick here, whilst dealing abroad?
Put them in prison for wanting to be well!
Teach them a lesson with a night in a cell!

Remove their liberty make them feel
Like a criminal for hurting nobody? It's like some
kind of hell!
Biz Ivol, Claire Hodges, Chris Baldwin and more
DIED feeling like Criminals so what's the score?

It's just a plant, tiny and pure,
That heals the sick. It does nothing more.
Stop locking up the sick
It's a victimless crime.

And there's much better ways to spend police time.
There's rapists and murderers
And violent thugs on the street.
But there's no policeman on the beat.

There are robberies and car thieves,
And hunters with dogs, there are paedophiles,
Groomers and people so vile,
That all need arresting and putting in jail.

Before you knock on a sick woman's door,
Look at this list and inspire for more
Than destroying a family who did nobody harm
And definitely don't own a cannabis farm.

If it wasn't so serious it might be funny.
To self medicate is a human right.
To lock up people with no victim
Is a right load of shite.

SMILE TIL THE END

Turn off the news
Turn off your tears
Turn off the hatred
Turn off your fears

Stop dropping bombs
Stop making war
Stop killing children
Stop please no more

Start being kind
Start making friends
Start making peace
Start making amends

Look for the good
Look for the people
They are your church
They are your steeple

Smile at your neighbour
Smile at a friend
Smile at a stranger
Smile till the end

WORDS

BY

JEZZA AUSTIN

I'm just a weird guy that walks his dawgs! taking pictures or writing words and sharing them on People in the North East on all social media. I smoke weed and enjoy life and love to share the hobby with everyone xx 4:20 For Life xx Nanoo Nanoo

http://peopleinthenortheast.co.uk/

DARKNESS TO AN UNKNOWN LAND

What is the darkness?
Where does it go?
These are the things that I really need to know!

But just when I feel I'm starting to understand
Here comes the darkness taking me to an unknown
land.
This land is my epilepsy to which I've no control
I just pray I'm not hurt when I start to fall

Though being epileptic isn't all that bad
It's the embarrassment that I feel that makes me really
sad.
Because people describe an inner demon that comes
out when I fit
And I find it really scary to even try to comprehend it

And just when I feel I am starting to understand
Here comes the darkness taking me to an unknown
land
This land is the depression the self loathing and the
doubt
This land of total darkness there is only one way out

So I ask myself the questions have I any fight left to give?
And I really do believe that I don't want to live.
So I gather all my tablets and take them one by one
And think to myself soon I will be gone!

That was twenty three years ago and here I still stand
And though I still see the darkness
No longer do I go to an unknown land....

MY POEM TO CANNABIS

Would you tell me that you loved me
If I said that I love you
Would you promise to stand by me
If I said my heart was true

Would you give me that warm feeling
When it's dark and cold outside
Will you promise to always lift me
When my poor old bones have died

Cannabis, cannabis my god I truly love you so
You used to be recreational…
But now that is no more
You bring me life, you bring me love,
You bring me hope I can go on
I may not be an athlete, but I feel like I belong.

They say that you are evil it will lead to harder things
But I found that it helps you appreciate, the small
Mercies that it brings
Like walking with no pain,
And my fits they ain't so bad

My life's screwed up but that's OK! because I don't
Feel sad I feel stoned I feel alive I feel content at last I
Feel hope I feel peace I feel Ive past the test
So come on life come what may I am here and I am
strong
As long as you come with cannabis
We will get along....

FRIENDSHIP

Someone asked me all about friendship
What it meant to me back then and now?
So I stopped and I thought all about it
And I started to explain how

Back then, We took it for granted
Back then, We partied none stop
Back then, We lived for today
Back then, We were on top!

And I sat and explained the difference
How time may have moved us all on
Some of us may have moved on forever
But that bond that we shared remains strong!

They say " You can't make new friends with old
friends"
Well I ain't sure that that's really right!
When you ain't seen those old friends forever
The reunion is like the very first night!

The friendship and love grow brighter
The memories and tears start to flow
The laughter just gets even louder
And new memories are starting to grow!

So in response to your very first question
From back then and right now
Is In my heart I've loved them for ever
But I just couldn't show them how....

ONLY DOING THE THINGS YOU LOVE!

I know I complain; about being in pain
But you see! pain is a big part of my life.
But what you may not know is what I'm thankful for
And what gives me the will to survive.

I start every day; out walking my dogs
As most are asleep in their beds.
Spliff in my mouth, Country music in my ears
Wishing I was back in mine instead.

I'm so fucking sore; I light my spliff to ignore
The hell as I walk on to the park.
I see the bairns play; and right then "life's okay"
Don't even mind that it's; pissing down and it's dark.

Then as I struggle back home; my thoughts starting to
roam
I wonder…. that's it! It's a photography day.
I can't wait to get explore; though not very far …
yes I know
And it's all worth the price; that I pay.

For the love of doing what I love; I suffer and moan
But to me! That's just what life's all about.
Enjoy it as much as you can; for as long as you have
Before your life's candle burns out....

Photo by Alun Buffry

WORDS

BY

ROCKY van de BENDERSKUM

Ex-tramp, Ex-teacher, writes poems and stuff Ex-tremely inappropriate and if that ain't enough, One thing for sure I'm too Punk to Funk. I don't drink booze so I never get drunk. Leukaemia Survivor and my spirit is strong, I know all the words can't remember the song. I love to scribble and write stuff like this I once stood for parliament. I reminisce I lived in the woods for a minute or two Natural born anarchist if that gives you a clue I fight for what's right and insist on the truth. Geriactivist and I'm long in the tooth

https://www.benderskum.rocks/

A STRANGE POEM

Strange to be normal when everything's weird
Strange that reality is all that we feared
Stranger than fiction, weirder than fact
Stranger than actors who simply, can't act
Strangely strange but oddly normal
Strangely naked while trying to be formal
Strange that I scribble cos I simply can't paint
Strange you believe that I'm something i ain't
Strange that to breathe becomes such a task
Strange it's ignored when I ask, ask and ask
Strange days are here as we've waited so long
Strange that an anthem is merely a song
Strange that the words were all simply wrong
Strange I'm so weak when I used to be strong
Strange to believe that we're not in great danger
Strange in the mirror there is only a stranger

ANARCHY IN THE UK

I say that I'm an Anarchist and this I do believe
The end is nigh for governments of this I can
conceive
A person who believes in or tries to bring about
anarchy
Is the dictionary definition but that makes no sense to
me
I say that I'm an Anarchist and this is what I mean
Don't want central government, dictator, king or
queen
My LANGUAGE might be savoury but I'm not a
fucking twat
 It doesn't mean I want to smash, or burn down this or
that
I'll always believe in freedom, and always will refrain
From smashing and burning everything cos that
would be insane
I believe that we could organise to efficiently meet
our needs
Without historic hierarchies born of war and greed
Anarchism wouldn't be the death of fair society
That's occurring every day with government
impropriety
They think that we're all stupid but this all has to stop
Just look at all the people at what is called the top
Anarchy isn't chaos but a gateway to autonomy
That's a nicer fucking model for building our
economy
With willing individual and active co-operation
We're on the better road to a truly human nation
Criminals, bankers, politicians and thieves
Wouldn't be able to do what they please

We'd govern locally with fully moral laws
Not distant unknown leaders with the usual age old
flaws
Everyone could have their say everyone a voice
No policing by coercion but governance through
choice
I understand confusion because it's what we've
learned
Controlling propaganda from media it gets churned
Another way to keep us down and to them it's just a
game
As a cannabis activist I've seen it loads and to me it's
all the same

AND THE CANNAFAM GROWS

The canna communities all met in a field
To combine our knowledge that's the weapon we
yield
Sheltering under a ruddy great tent
We speak of laws that are blatantly bent
Nutritional, Medicinal, Sacramental, Industrial and
Recreational
We talk about a plant that's quite simply sensational
We meet as friends uniting our cause
Seeking ways to remove their broken laws
That state if we grow it's a criminal act
While for big pharma they grow tons and that's a fact
In acres of greenhouses in Norfolk and Kent
Did I mention the laws that are blatantly bent?
In the rest of the world prohibition has stopped
travelling
As its lies are revealed and the truth is unravelling
The war on cannabis is totally political
The fact it continues here, is quite hypocritical
Canna corporations are standing in line
While prohibitionists watch their ethos decline
We Know Our Roots so the tide is now turning
As we spread our truths to the general public
everyone is learning

BRIBES AND BACKHANDERS

Whilst rumours abound over our complicity
Let me explain in plain simplicity
Tobacco and Big Pharma can sit and fucking wait
The thing I'll never do for you is bow down and
capitulate
Fuck off now with your dirty mountains of cash
We ain't your fucking puppets or is that a tad too
brash
Nobody pays us; we do it on our own
You could offer it to my face or call me on the phone
Quite simply, there's no figure that you could bribe
me with
You say you're honest businessmen but you sound a
lot like spivs
I've watched you for a while now and see how you
try to divide
None of us would be able to win this alone but at least
we fucking tried
My friends are all people of honour and never the
type to hide
But were accused of accepting your dosh in a
statement that simply lied
There is no truth or foundation in statements such as
this
So fuck your accusations because they simply boil my
piss

CANNABIS IS SCHEDULE ONE

Cannabis is schedule one but if you know, you know
that's dumb
Medicinal properties it has none well that's if it's
really schedule one

Everyone knows that this law sucks
but the government here could give two fucks

They'll make it legal, when they make money
but for those who are ill, this just ain't funny

So we'll descend en masse, to parliament square
and try to make the government care

Give us our meds is all we ask.
Is that such a terribly difficult task

But if they don't give us what we need
the rights to our meds and to grow our seed

When it's time to vote, remember this.
You'll be at the bottom of our list

MEDUCATION

When they heard of a plant that grew like a weed,
with the most nutritious edible seed,
Its medicinal properties were second to none, with
thousands of uses and then still some.
If used for bricks it's a carbon sink that could clean up
the air did that make them think,
Could be spun into fabric for clothes and more, well
at least that's how it was before.
No, they made it illegal to own or consume and don't
plant that seed it's illegal to bloom
So now they just follow an ancient lie, it's a
dangerous drug so they'll pass it by,
Medicinal value it has none, so that's why they put it
in schedule one.
A bunch of lies, not an inkling of truth that they hold
onto now despite all the proof.
Now they grow it themselves with complete
autonomy yet deny it to us...how can that be?
They care about profit and they're lying to you but
isn't that what they always do
They ignore the truth while changing the rules and
believe we are just a bunch of fools
Historically they told everyone it was bad but that
bubble has burst and that makes me glad
The world is much wiser than it was way back when
and soon we'll have medicine growing again,
Out in the open where it ought to be not hidden in
closets but proud and free,
And on that day I'll stand and smile we'll have won
the fight but it's been quite a while.

CBDBDBD

Looking at lots of recent news I've noticed a different trend
Media talking about cannabis like prohibition is going to end
But I also see another side and this is what worries me
A push for synthetic cannabinoids developed in factories
Or maybe a laboratory made in a Petri dish
Something quite abhorrent and smelling worse than fish
And then I hear from some vendors of hemp and CBD
Saying 'Our stuff will not get you high' but that's not the point to me
They vilify the THC. The Helpful Cannabinoid
Every time I hear that shit, it gets me quite annoyed
With THC and the full entourage the difference is clearly massive
Without it your Endocannabinoid system will only be working on passive
My research tells me that CBD blocks CB2 transmitters
So when excluding the THC you are merely counterfeiters
I agree that CBD has a place amongst the full entourage
But ignoring the other cannabinoids is clearly sabotage
So kindly stop your rhetoric it really isn't funny
Or carry on telling your big fat lies and rake in your dirty money

I know not all the vendors are here just to make a buck
But those of you who are doing that I hope you run out of luck
They'll sell you oil that's only fit to fry a couple of eggs
They're the ones I'm talking about and they really are the dregs
There are many honest vendors and some I know quite well
And then there spivs who would sell their own kids to make their profits swell
So I hope all you honest vendors will listen to what I just said
Get rid of the line 'Ours Won't Get You High' and put that shit to bed
It was invented by clever spin doctors to keep prohibition in place
Then passed to unscrupulous people who would clearly lie to your face
And I know that CBD can be good and some people sell it with pride
But for those of us with cancer and stuff it would not even touch the sides
But knowledge is spreading and people are waking
I hope all of you can soon be partaking
With decriminalised cannabis use available to all
The taxes from sales just wouldn't be small
It could make lots of money for our struggling NHS
And bring other revenue in to help all the rest
Billions to help our crumbling economy
Grow Your Own to help everyone's autonomy

With Climate crisis life as we know is very much in
peril
The end of society is looming and soon everything
will be feral
While governments ignore the facts and the truth
Even when they are shown indisputable proof
Hemp in the fields for food, oil and more
Ending the need for another world war
But how did we come to be in such a stew
Don't look at your history books they lie to you too
The people in charge are a tiny percent
And they are blatantly crooked twisted and bent
They own all the media and keep governments in
their pockets
They act like they're aliens who came here in some
rockets
OK I realise that's a stretch of the facts
So I'll bid you adieu in my tin foil hat

BENDERSKUM THOUGHTS

Did you feel bloated on Christmas day? I hope not
much food was thrown away
I know it was though it's always like that and the one
percent's wallets still get fat
While down at the bottom and out on the street there
are very many people that can't afford to eat
Now this is a fact a cast iron truth it's really fucking
hard when you live by nail and tooth
I know cos I have been there and seen it through these
eyes there's more to life than 9 to 5 that's slavery in
disguise
My life outside the boundaries made me look way far
beyond and I know it is quite hard to think like that in
this totally clogged up pond
My life outside the boundaries was hard but it was
free and if I'd never lived it I doubt that I'd be me
In the winter all my clothing would be frosted to the
floor
But soon enough with a spliff in my gob I'd make the
burner roar
In just my boots I'd hang my clothes above it in the
heat, lucky for me I lived deep in the woods and not
on a city street
If you live on the streets it's just as cold and probably
colder still cos you won't have a home-made wood
burner to take away the chill
So living on the streets was not a choice for me
because I'm a born survivor and know what it is to be
free
Not something I intended not something I had

planned but this could happen to anyone I hope you
understand
I used to work with gardens and trees and I really
loved my job and quite a few bits of dangerous work
but I earned a fair few bob
One night my vehicle and tools were taken that
fucked my work couldn't bring home the bacon
Well being a veggie that wasn't too bad and as for the
rest well, it could've been sad
I lived in a nice flat full of my stuff and sold it all for
a ton then watched him struggle to carry it out and
smiled when it was done
I travelled round the country I even went to France
well I actually woke up on a train by some strange
circumstance
I went into town to a hippy bar someone put
something in my drink well that's how I ended up
there in France is all I can think
I got nicked in Ostend for being rude to an ugly bloke
a uniformed dude
I wasn't that rude just having some fun then he got
quite pissed off and pointed his gun
Which made me laugh more. Oh! It has to be said at
this point in my life I was out of my head
I sang Hari Krishna with my hands on my head which
angered him more his face went bright red
The more I laughed the worse it got the dude and his
mate were losing the plot
A crowd starts to form and a cop car arrives out from
the car jumps an officer guy

I had machine pistols prodding my ribcage but
decided the gorillas were bluffing

On reflection I guess it was lucky for me the new
guy's hobby was cuffing
Much to the displeasure of the red faced buffoons
their officer arrived to relieve them too soon
So there was I in a car with some cops its gets far far
worse it just never stops
They said there had been a burglary and they thought
it might be me
But I didn't fit the description so soon they let me free
Maybe you only just guessed maybe you knew all
along my life was little bit sketchy back then like a
dodgy 80s song
So somehow I came to my senses or maybe I deeper
dug I loved my herb as I always have but danced to
another drug
Went to many raves with a pill seller my lost best
friend Yella
With me nearby looking mean as fuck it looked like I
was the fella.

Can you imagine me looking mean as fuck? Not these
days baby you're out of luck
In a car I travelled in style for a while with a girl and
we lived in my tent
She simply did my head in with tarot and I ended up
living in Kent
Doing my head in, how could that be? A reading, for
how do you want your tea?

So I moved to a place called Penny Pot Wood and I
lived very simply as I knew that I could
That's when I found the place where I belong but that
my dears is another fucking song

EXTINCTION

It gives us everything we need,
Somewhere to live and thrive and succeed
It gives us plants it gives us trees,
Fertile lands and wondrous seas
But the human virus is the worst disease
And we've brought this planet to its knees
We've stripped away lots and put back a bit
As for biodiversity we don't give a shit
They tell us we've only got 12 years NO more
To sort it all out and even the score
But in my opinion it's too little too late
Those horses have bolted through the open gate
Just like a virus moving into a cell
We are making our planet a living hell
When we've used up everything that we can see
I expect we'll be hoping for 'Planet B'
When I look at my world I just shed a tear
Cos most of you fuckers don't want to hear
You recycle plastic and paper and tins
And what can't be reused goes in landfill bins
But is that enough as our world starts to die
No just drive your car and continue to fly
I'm doing my bit I cannot do more
Blah, blah, blah I've heard it before
The world can repair itself of that there's no doubt
But we won't be here to sing, talk or shout
We'll be long gone extinct like the dinosaur
Without the effects of a giant meteor
It won't be too long till we're buried in plastic
PLEASE listen to this these words aren't bombastic
We are using our planet as a means to an end

But when something is broken it's important to mend
There are holes in the sky where radiation gets in
And when it does it will burn your skin
Because these holes are fat while our atmospheres thin
The holes were all made by human pollution
So to clean up our act is the sensible solution
We can't keep on taking without putting back
When it's empty it's empty and that is a fact
Were cutting down trees, polluting air, sea and soil
And surprise, surprise we're addicted to oil
That particular oil comes from way underground
But there's other oil that is easily found
For there is a plant with wondrous seeds
That can help us and all of our planetary needs
We have never needed fossil oils
They pollute our atmosphere and seas and soils
There is a plant with amazing yields
That we could be planting in our fields
Our planet is fragile we don't need to break her
There's oil from this plant 300 gallons an acre
As if that's not enough to make oil companies sour
After extraction there's 6 tons of flour
And medicine, building blocks and all sorts of things,
Eco safe plastic and paper and string
The list is quite endless as you'll quickly see
But what is that plant what could it be?
The plants name is cannabis but don't be alarmed
It's been here forever and it's not here to harm
It's been here forever it followed us round
It could clean up the air and puts food in the ground
So why don't we use this to help with our needs

The answer is simply put corporate greed
They made it illegal to own or consume
But I don't believe them and won't dance to their tune
They tell us its bad and say it's a pest
While hidden in plain view feather their nests
So heed what is said and grow all those seeds
Or just sit and watch telly as our home planet bleeds
So pretend that I'm lying when I say all this stuff
Cos to hear and ignore is really too tough
Our world is in peril there may be no next bit
No 'Planet B' and certainly no exit
Bill Hicks once called us a virus with shoes
So just keep consuming and I'll sing the blues

HYPOCRISY DEMOCKERACY

I smoked weed at uni the prime minister joked
While a legal hemp farm has its licence revoked
The crop was ready to harvest quite soon
But they weren't millionaires didn't have a silver spoon
Yet in Norfolk and Kent is a place where they grow
Tons of the stuff because they're in the know
Or is it because their licence is protected
While everyone else will get theirs rejected
They say it will be legal in fifteen years
So I don't understand why everyone cheers
That is way too long for many folks
I smoked cannabis in uni the prime minister jokes
So what about us lot if it's OK for those?
For us it's illegal and that's just how it goes
We grow Cannabinoids inside us it's true
So if growing's illegal you're criminals too
Along with all vertebrates all over the Earth
To the day they die from the moment of birth
Clinical Endocannabinoid Deficiency Syndrome (CECD)
Very long words too clever for me
When a child has its medicine taken you say that's not right
 But that's not the end of it this is everyone's fight
Some people just want it to chill and relax
They know this is true but they ignore the facts
Some want it for food some when they're ill
Without all the side effects from taking a pill
Some want it for clothing some want it to build

Did I mention that some of us just want to be chilled?
But the plants not illegal just so you know
It's illegal to own it, or sell it or grow
We all have a right to homeostasis
Not lost in a desert with no hope of oasis

Now the CannaFams from the tribal gatherings
Are strutting their stuff there are movements and
happenings
We realise for them it's all about money
But people are dying and that's just not funny
We do what we do not for fortune or fame
People are dying and it isn't a game
There are people in power who could end it today
But a dying child's mother can just sit and pray
This is the tragedy of Cannabis Prohibition
People are dying but our leaders don't listen

LEGAL LIES

Luxembourg has legalised
Remove 5 letters that leaves Lies
It tightens the law and makes it much stronger
So those who rebel will suffer for longer

If you do not follow their very strict rules
They are ready and waiting like blue clad ghouls
They don't even care if you're 13 or seventy
Because now you're a criminal and not just peasantry

They have followed these lies for so many years they
now think they follow the truth
Whilst keeping their eyes shut to global change and
continually ignoring the proof
The next bit is possibly a bit of a joke or maybe a
glimpse of the future
We'd best not sit still or it could become truth and
need much more to fix than a suture

There are entrepreneurs poised and ready to pounce
Wait for it Britain the one thousand pound ounce
You may think that funny but just hear me out as a
long time drug war survivor
What you willingly pay someone twenty five quid for,
not long ago cost just a fiver

I don't like our government you may well have guessed
But then I'm an Anarchist and I don't like the rest
Governments that is, from all over the worlds what I mean

What I'd prefer is autonomy not some bullshit money
regime

Uruguay has three and a half million citizens but
legalising is done and dusted
They have twenty legal selling points any others stand
the chance to get busted
So legalisation isn't the way it's a lie with a new set
of rules
And yet still they peddle that tired old shite they
really must think we are fools

Decriminalise, and de-schedule cannabis it isn't what
I'd call rocket science
 And don't start making fake activist groups and offer
to form an alliance
We've spotted you before and we'll spot you again
And we haven't become stupider than we were way
back when

Prohibition was invented a hundred years or so back
So it's time that it went let's not seek another track
So government just surrender it's a failed drug war
Nobody believes what you say it's there for

Don't promise to change it if I vote for your lot
Do I have faith in your word? I believe I do not
It's just all merely rhetoric and can soon be ignored
I've seen more integrity, trust, from any old horse on
a skateboard

MASTERS OF DEFLECTION

What ever pretty colour your party's rosette is,
I hope that you soon realise they all just take the piss
They aren't here for you and certainly not for me
But why they are is perfectly clear to stay at the top of
the tree
You may feel this all seems simply quite abrupt
But then most politicians are simply quite corrupt
A leading politician decided to cross the road
Then claimed eighty quid expenses the thieving
fucking toad
I admit that that's a joke of course it is you see I'm
not a liar
Eighty quid was just a start the claim would be much
higher

A day or so it seems in the working life of a lord
 Is to fall asleep on a leather seat the result of
becoming bored
A day in the life of a common for surely that's what
they are
 Despite the fancy houses and chauffeur driven cars
Is meant to be what they promised when they stood in
a general election
But this is something hard to miss they are masters of
deflection
They all have their own agendas and continue them
when they are able
While the promises they made just to get your vote
aren't even under the table
So this is a reason why anarchy is superior to this at
present

I'm not even distantly royal no but I'm still not a
fucking peasant
I believe in the people's autonomy
Not this crippled lop-sided economy

There once a great depression that wasn't so great I'm
sure
An era when nobody had any work that ended up in a
war
But it's all just manipulation, a means to an end or
horses for courses
The workers were there and the factories and
whodathunkit the natural resources
So if you think my hats made of tin and all this stuff
is just in my head
Do the maths, look at the facts and carefully think
about what I just said
There was once a great depression it ended in a war
But the infrastructure to facilitate it were already
there before

What ever pretty colour your party's rosette is,
Now have you figured out they all just take the piss
Homelessness. The poor or people who just aren't
healthy
Not really on the agenda cos that won't keep them
wealthy

All of my life I've watched our world get sold from
under our feet
The owners now the oligarchs and political elite
Digging it up knocking it down to overload a purse

Destroying what once was beautiful nothing could be
worse
We live in an autocracy although they call it a
democracy
 But everyone knows that's a filthy lie and maybe
even hypocrisy
So instead of keep on asking for things that are
already yours
Demand the end of this status quo and to change their
fucking laws

Or do your things in spite of them either will get you
my applause

So rouse a politician, wake it from its sleep
Say it's time to get a job and leave the leather seat

NO VICTIM NO CRIME

There's nothing subliminal, I'm just not a criminal
At least not for grass, it's the law that's an arse
I'm a painter and I've used that stuff for over 40 years,
I'm not fucking crazy and still have both of my ears
Cannabis for me relieves my constant pain,
Without me feeling that I've gone completely insane
It helps with my pain so then I am able to paint
But a gateway drug? That's something which it ain't
They announced medicinal legality to the general
population
But if you know, you know that's bullshit information
But for me it's not just medicine it's my pleasure and so
very much more
As a Cantheist I felt… sort of blessed each time I was
able to score
Now an end to prohibition would be the best cessation
Medical, recreational, spiritual and more, one people
under one nation
And the freedom to grow whatever the use a positive
culmination
But friends and family of top politicians grow cannabis
with no intention of pausing
Whilst people are still getting busted the police are still
kicking their doors in
They grow acres and acres but deny it to us
Then it shouldn't surprise them that we make such a fuss
Keeping hold of their monopoly is all they really care
for
Hiding behind ancient hypocrisy unfortunately our
current drug law
So if a law is unworkable and clearly seen to be broken
If you broke it again would it fix it or is that just my
optimist joking

MIRACLES AND LIES

Is it any wonder that people get so lyrical
When they speak out loud of this medical miracle
Recreational, industrial or even sacramental
To make that all illegal is nothing short of mental
Governments come and governments go
But this is a fact everyone should know
Whilst most Cannabis remains at schedule one
That they leave it that way is not just dumb
But maybe something a lot more sinister
Just look at the husband of our former Drugs Minister
Maintaining a law that's criminally insane
At the same time as making personal gain
It's time that this ended and they freed the weed
And left me alone to grow my own seed

PHARMALOONICALS

Greetings to all you listeners I'm a rhyming
storyteller
If it ever went to print it would never be a best seller
We are not a traditional person and don't have
multiple personalities
I'd like to make that point quite clear and be done
with all the formalities
While lying down in hospital full of pharmaceuticals
All my hair fell out and my nails and my cuticles
I wasn't really that surprised with my body so full of
poison
My skin was scaled like lizards but I simply couldn't
moisten
I'm now allergic to everything, which is a total
fucking pain
From certain nuts, to sunshine and acid in the rain
I still take some of it daily of this you may be shocked
Due to side effects of chemo that left my lungs quite
blocked
I daily inhale powder straight into my lungs
I also vape my cannabis but that is much more fun
I had a ton of chemo which has left my body quite
broken
But my smile sits like the Cheshire cat of this I'm
sure I've spoken
There is a thing called chemo-brain of which you may
have heard
Our brains control our bodies but mine is quite absurd
With taste buds that are almost gone enjoy food I do
not
And chocolate burns like chilli and quite a fucking lot
My Endocannabinoid system could help with all of

this
But it is often quite deficient due to lack of cannabis
I've seen some clever doctors who know about this
stuff
But they are tied to pharma rules so can never do
enough
So to really make a difference some things would
have to change
That isn't going to happen so why is this not strange?
The pharmaceuticals companies prefer this status quo
We need to have a turnaround prohibition needs to go
We need an honest government to remove these
biased laws
That's not the government that we have unfortunately
cos they're corporate fucking whores
Until then I'll break the law a criminal I'll remain
I'll never believe the government because they're
criminally insane
Or maybe they're just greedy as they make a lot of
cash
Locking away us criminals for cannabis flowers and
hash
This infrastructure suits them so prohibition stays
If you really knew the truth of it I think you'd be
amazed
I've been a criminal my whole adult life so a criminal
I remain
But with my daily cannabis use they say I should be
quite insane
They sent me off to hospital to a neurological
psychiatrist
Who diagnosed that I'm totally sane but here's the

fucking twist

They are all in the thrall of big pharma it's them who pay the bills

So even though I'm as sane as her, she tried to give me pills

If you say you like my poems but grimace at my profanities

Apologies, but they will continue till we end such pharma insanities

So now we wait for prohibition to end and it's been a bit of a while

My body continues to fall to bits

And Yet I Fucking Smile

PROHIBIOHAZARD

When I reminisce on my life I can't help but think
I simply love cannabis I'm glad I don't drink
I've always used cannabis and not just a bit
It will make me go crazy is a big pile of shit
A head shrinking doctor declared me quite sane
And agreed that cannabis was good for my brain
It's good for my brain and good for my body
Unlike the pharma shit that's really quite shoddy
There will surely come a time when the people aren't
enslaved
Perhaps they'll try to understand how our leadership
behaved
Prohibition is my enemy it's never been my friend
If I let it get to me it'll drive me round the bend
I'm out here in the open and still I won't pretend
Prohibition is my enemy it's never been my friend
Our lovely world is broken cannabis could help the
mend
Prohibition is the enemy it's never been our friend
300 gallons of oil from a single acre field
Now that' s what I call a phenomenal fucking yield
You may well have thunk a think so already you
decided
That I'm a foul mouthed nutter or simply just
misguided
Or maybe you think I talk lots of sense
 I'm not really one to sit on the fence
My fight will continue until it relents
In this broken drug war I hope to make some dents

Cannabis amazes me I'll shout from the roof
It's helping with my hurting and that is just my truth
Prohibition is the enemy it's never our friend
I'm out here in the open and still I won't pretend
I've done all this for years and I'll do it all some more
Blah, blah, blah, blah, blah, blah, blah, I'm sure you
know the score

SMILE

I realise it all seems quite grim right now and looks to
be getting worse
How did our people give us what seems like another
five years of this curse?
And I'm not really sure how I got this drawn in
As an anarchist I usually ignore all that spin
But chin up folks what happened is done I guess we
should batten the hatches
When society is failing mistrust gets built up with an
infrastructure made out of patches
So try not to worry although you may due to recently
unbalanced thingummy
This may be the end but that's also the start and so on
but so surreptitiously
Nothing is forever or guaranteed really but birth and
life and death
So try to be happy and smile in its face till it takes its
very last breath
If you aren't royal stock or at least upper crust
As far as they're concerned you can all just eat dust
If you've managed to get this far into this drone
Even though I continue in this monotonous tone
What I'm trying to tell you is just not a moan
I forgot I wasn't actually talking to String
My imaginary friend…Now there's a thing
As I said just before it's really quite grim so there's
only one way it can go
So look up look around and get rid of the frown try to
smile you may not feel so low

I've had chemo galore and bone marrow transplant
that's just in case you dint know
I really meant didn't cos the other sort is a hollow and
the after effect of a blow
So here I am telling you the same sort of stuff as most
of those witchy girls tell
Beware of my locks or my tickety tocks they could
maybe put you under my spell
But this nonsense I spout always keeps me amused
And if you don't get my drift you'll just be confused
But I drift from the point if you know what it was if
you didn't well neither did I
But it got you distracted and listening to nonsense and
maybe a smile in your eye
So take hope from it all as it isn't all bad
And I realise you may feel you've all just been had
I'm just the same I got drawn into this game and
those who to blame
Are politically insane and not worth my breath to
utter their names
So try to keep smiling and take heart from my words
Or dismiss what I say and just think I'm absurd
If you do then I'll think that you just never heard
That adversity is just a calamitous event
So then smile at it all because that's what I meant
As division of all of us is there final intent
Democracy is crooked and broken and bent
So a new ideology is clearly what's needed
Get rid of your anger or they have succeeded
Instead fill your heart with love for this earth
The place where you live this land of our birth

And I'm not meaning country when I speak of this
land
It's the big wider world and it's really quite grand
The world that's in peril that needs a strong hand
So please stop the squabbling and just make a stand
Please stop all the hatred it's really quite vile
You're my brothers and sisters and I urge you to smile
It's sad the hate that I am seeing
This from another…human…being
Things seem quite grim but they have for a while
My health's not improving…and yet I still smile

JUST WALK ON BY

I hope that soon my actions will be freed
Although I continue to throw my seed
For the birds to eat or maybe to grow
That's the wonder of nature you just never know
If you do see one growing there's no need to report it
If you first do some research you may find you
support it
Some use it for medicine some just for pleasure
Some use it spiritually and believe it's a treasure
Its potential is boundless believe me it's true
So don't phone the police it's not hurting you
The council will be called to cut that plant down
Those Horticidal Maniacs just make me frown
If you did a little research then maybe you'd find
It's good for so much and that might change your
mind
It's good for the planet, our health and much more
It could save them a fortune on their failed drug war
It costs thousands and thousands to make a drug sting
For only three hours that's fact, it's a thing
Hundreds of police and thousands of hours
But not only drugs, hash or cannabis flowers
Also knives, guns and ammo and all sorts of loot
The organised crime gangs are not afraid to shoot
After just a few hours shots will be heard
And this is the reason the drug war's absurd
With the organised crime gang arrested and gaoled
A new gang moves in and the drug war has failed
Without prohibition there's no need for a sting
Because organised crime would be less of a thing

It all really started with alcohol
But that's freely available as we already know
If you go into town on Saturday night
You'll find many drunken people who just want to
fight
In 1920 or round about that time
Prohibition gave birth to organised crime
When they banned all that booze and closed all the
bars
The criminals delivered in lorries and cars
It made honest citizens suddenly turn bad
For the want of a thing that they previously had
But criminals are often called entrepreneurs
Soon they had booze sold behind their locked doors
When one place was busted they opened another
Because of organised crime and they were its Mother
They became quite powerful. Really quite feared
The alcohol ban ended but they never disappeared
They were organised now and intended to stay
They could make lots of money with no taxes to pay
But ending the failed war on drugs would at least
Take a chunk of their empire and diminish the beast
Some changes need making all this needs to stop
Don't start at the bottom though, start at the top
There are people in power who profit from crime
So this status quo for them is sublime
They're as bad as the criminals but never do time
With Diogenes' lamp in the darkest of places
They'd be quite invisible if you shone it in their faces
Once more I digress from the subject at hand
So why not grow cannabis in my mother land?
You first need a license? And that is the key

The husband of one of them has a near monopoly
It is no big secret they do what they please
They grow it and harvest then sell it with ease
So then if they can do it with no song and dance
We ought to be able to grow our own plants
But they really don't want us to be so enlightened
The loss of their profit is what gets them frightened

NO TO YOUR BAD LAW

As I' m a lifelong gardener and I love to grow my
plants
I would grow my medicine if given half a chance
I could grow my own sacrament for my very spiritual
needs
I could do lots and lots of things if I could grow my
seeds
I could grow for myself and grow for my mates
And even have cannabis cake on my plates
But the law says I can't so I'll answer again
When you ask me these questions whilst I grimace in
pain
Are you disabled? It's hard to say
Are you in pain? Just everyday
Will it get better? I think it will not
Does anything help? Illegal Pot
So why is it illegal if it helps with your pain?
You could ask my government, but I think they're
insane
Although in fact nowadays it's just a tad worse
They are heavily invested chapter and verse
Giving out licenses to family and friends
But they are the lawmakers so it's their law that bends
They make millions in profit from their cannabis
monopoly
So they won't give it up and give me autonomy
They are making a fortune with cannabis prohibition
So challenging that is my focus, my mission

So hear me prohibitionists, in your stuffed leather
seats
You are losing this war on my actions so you'd better

sound your retreat
I declare that your Misuse of Drugs Act is really not
fit for purpose
Although you are morally bankrupt you use it just to
usurp us
And the way it's enforced is nowhere near fair
Depending on if you live here, here or there
I denounce your bad laws that declare me a criminal
I'm not fucking guilty. How's that for subliminal?
None of my actions will cause any harm
I'm calling an end to your war so disarm
No Victim No Crime is something that's said
Your Laws can Fuck Off let that enter your head

THE NOOSE

There are many who don't want decriminalised weed
No puff, puff, pass or growing our seed
They're too deeply rooted in corporate greed
To allow us to have our actions freed
That beautiful plant with the palmate leaves
With so many uses you wouldn't believe
Whose oil can help make seizures cease
Or at very least seem to vastly decrease
For Homeostasis its nutrition is tops
It should be 'A' listed a 'Number One Crop'
And what is wrong with a chilling smoke
With these outdated laws it's an unfunny joke
But we'll keep on fighting for everyone's use
Smoke, vape, eat, build, wear or even make juice
I hope all the factions can just call a truce
Prohibition is the enemy bad laws are the noose

THE HORROR OF IT ALL

I don't have a very sound body; it's broken and full of
disease
Everyone knows I'm an anarchist and I'll never get
down on my knees
I protest whenever I'm able I lobby in parliament too
But the problem with that is I'm not a big cat
And parliaments just like a zoo
The government here is a fucking disgrace
They look down their noses and lie to your face
Smug politicians think its all funny cos the more
people die must make them money
But their days must be numbered I hope that that's
true
I've been watching the media and seen something
new
I don't want to argue or get into fights; I just want
what's fair <u>for all</u> Human Rights
There's homeless and poverty and foodbanks and war
there's fracking, pollution and just so much more
There's toffee nosed arseholes who sit on plush seats
whilst every day people die on our streets
I'm a cannabis activist and have been for years but I
look at my world and my eyes fill with tears
So I urge you to think and don't pass on by and settle
for what is obviously a lie
I just want to paint and do beautiful things but how
can I do that with the horror this brings

AUSTERITY

We don't have to live with right wing austerity
And whether or not you like my poetry
This you need to know before it's too late
There is a way to put ample on everybody's plate
To be a billionaire you must have something missing
And don't be mistaken it's not rich people that I'm
dissing
I admire quite openly folks, who've made a fortune
from their work
Though I'll never have such luxury I'm not the sort to
shirk
I've never wanted riches just enough to live with ease
To leave me free to scribble and pay my worldly fees
But back to that austerity a very unnecessary blight
On everyone who isn't rich and it isn't fucking right
It was invented by those in power just like the great
depression
And never should have started a totally evil
transgression
When people die on our streets and most people just
walk by
Any hope of moral decency is merely pie in the sky
The far right are rising again has history taught us
nothing?
Just like the rise of the Nazis this lot are not bluffing
Hospital beds aren't empty they have simply
disappeared
As our world is changing for the worse something we
all should fear
The climate is changing its getting quite bad of which

many seem not to have noticed
Believing instead the lies they are fed by the people
whose plates are quite bloated
These are worrying times for the sick and disabled
and children and doctors and nurses
If I named all the people who it's worrying for I'd
need many, many more verses
But even the dragon-like billionaires will eventually
end up in hearses
You are born, go to school then it's soon time to work
and you'll do this until you are dead
Well at least if retirement age gets much later and I'm
quite sure that's something they've said
They say they've created a lot of new jobs, some
people have two jobs or more
But with minimum wage and zero hours contracts
those poor folks will always be poor
I've got a confession that my facial expression
Hides behind it some pent-up aggression
But it isn't just me there's a rising tide and it's
spreading across the globe
For me it started deep down inside but it's now in my
frontal lobe
We have to do something or what kind of world will
be left to pass on to our young
As I said just before there is change in the air and I
hope that it's truly begun
Cuts to social services and hospitals and schools
The fire brigade, police and more they really think
we're fools
Although perhaps they could be right as the masses
seem to follow

No! I don't believe their rhetoric it's too bitter a pill to
swallow
So what can we do to open your eyes?
Because everything they say is clearly lies
Thinly veiled deceit almost without a disguise
Are you really blind to the fact it's us that they
despise
It saddens me when I hear of the fact
Many species are extinct so there's no going back
Sixty percent of the Earth's animal population
Have gone since the seventies is no exaggeration
The seas are rising and they are full of plastic
We need to do something and something quite drastic
If you really can't see it then maybe you're blind
Or totally stupid and that's me being kind

DIMETHYLTRYPTAMINE

Transcendental almost mental
Treading paths previously untrodden or merely just
forgotten
Forbidden truths from eye and tooth without the proof
Taking a long hard lingering look into the minds
inexorable book
I'll huff and I'll puff but it's all just stuff
Wherever will it come to an end? Over here over
there or just around the bend
Or perhaps with luck even further yet or is that a state
of patience impossible to get
Impossible for the naked mind to behold without
being bold and permitting your mind to really unfold
Curling around that wonderful infinitesimal sound
removing your clothing to feel the ground
Touching the universe being the earth wondrous
sensation in the place of our birth
But it's broken and burned nature unturned is this
really the extent to what we have learned?
It seems we have remembered very little and thus our
lives have become very brittle
Ready to fall back out from this trip but is that really
it?

THE PANTRY OF DOOM

The pantry of doom
The harbour of gloom
Alone in the dark and it feels like your tomb
Death is inevitable and won't come too soon
But then as usual it's gonna be late
Move over death you have to wait
But that's not really a thing that you ought to hate
And certainly not a subject that you need to debate
So another day another dollar
So you scream so you holler
How can you be living in this unbearable squalor?
Waiting for the man to come and feel your collar
He'd take you in, lock you away
So you wouldn't have to pray
At least not until another lonely darkened day
But then again it suddenly might all go away

THE RAILWAY HOTEL, SOUTHEND ON SEA

Vegan Pizza in an Essex pub
Lovely Scran rub a dub, dub
Rub a dub reggae 'Know Your Roots'
But the law of the land means none of those zoots
But one day soon, you never know
Though for now it's illegal so it just don't show
Chay running around taking the pics
Using 'Gaffa' the tape flags to fix
Owen, Rachel, Paul and me
Orange juice and pizza plenty for tea
I tried to decipher all the legalese
But that stuffs corrupt seems complicated to me
But I made a good contact to help me with this
He proper knows this stuff so his input is bliss
Cakes and stuff passing around
Wonderful people amazing sounds
Everyone chilling no sign of grief
Canna Famial it beggars belief
I bought someone a cake he couldn't believe his eyes
Luckily he didn't suss my undercover disguise
But then what I needed was a proper cup of tea
Black and sweet, lo and behold it appeared in front of me
Diversity of folks some old, some new
Some a tad coked up but none were sniffing glue
Thumping reggae and the odd drum or two
Some people looking for something to do
One way street parked back to front
Who parked that there what a silly…way to park
Sitting in amongst it all writing in my book
Every now and then I gets very suspicious looks
Some think I'm writing poetry but I assure I am not

Just a load of words that rhyme on account of all that pot
Then going to the bog the door I could not find
A bloke appeared from nowhere I asked if he'd be so kind
To tell me where he came from am I so far out of my mind
So the difference is OH between mushies and DMT
If you just look at the genetics you will plainly see
A girl takes off her top then sniffs her underarms
Catches sight of me laughing enjoys my grinning charms
Sebastian asleep on a bar stool how cool can that lad be
Totally skilled individual seems proper awesome to me
A very pretty couple were grooving to the tune
The way that they were moving they ought to get a room
But my shift would soon be over in my undercover assignment
Then back to the office in Whitehall for a final draft refinement
Then another barstool sleeper a proper sight to see
Totally amazing balance how can that even be?
A stunning red haired beauty proper made me stare
She may have looked like French resistance but completely unaware
Good to see you Conner as she tripped upon your bag
A very wicked chat up line you very nearly had
When the group of aggie bouncers arrive it weren't to have no fun
Time to leave, move along your evenings completely done
So that's the end of this tale I tell
Of a lovely evening in the Railway Hotel.

CORONA, CORONA THE GOVERNMENT OWNS YA

There were lots of protests all across the world
About corrupted governments accusations being hurled
So to thwart this free thinking a new plan unfurled
In France we heard they had the yellow vests
Their government's policies were the worst not the best
Then a virus suddenly appeared in a market place in china
A way to stop the protesting world and a very dangerous definer
Then along came the people in their tin foil hats
Conspiracies on the cause was it this or maybe that
Some people said it was made in a laboratory
Some said it was copied from a little known horror story
That some blamed the Chinese was clearly defamatory
Announcement by world leaders were merely preparatory
Some said the governments were using it to take back their control
Estimations were in millions to be the final death toll
Some maybe suffocated by stockpiled bog roll
There were many mentions of thirty three
A number connected to the top of the tree
A Diophantine equation as hard as can be
$A^3 + B^3 + C^3$ will equal thirty three
It is used a lot by Mason's and in sacred geometry

The virus they say was deliberately made and also has a patent
While the basis of truth is hidden from us the result however is blatant
The anagram of corona virus turned out to be carnivorous
But it came from soup containing bat is just a bit ridiculous
That last sentence was very odd due to some of the words I will bet
But finding a place in a rhyme for bot is something I haven't done yet
So what can we do to make ourselves safe isn't the answer obvious itself?
For a start don't go stockpiling stuff leave that shit on the shelf
Wash your hands is what seems expert advice
So everyone does it and doesn't think twice
Hanitizer sales have gone through the roof that stuffs never been so popular
Remember though with that expert advice the importance of seems as the copular
For they really don't know any more than you
The difference is scary because it's something new

CORONADEBT

They called it yes they called it, they told us it was
coming
But because of cuts it overtook we were walking it
was running
At first they tried to convince us to build up herd
immunity
But if the vulnerable all died off it's a cash saving
opportunity
You may think they have your interests at heart
But they cocked it up right from the start
When you realise the government is lying to you
that's called apprehension
 But if you think they have a bloody clue you haven't
been paying attention
There's a corona bloody virus and it's got us all
locked down
The shops and things are mostly shut in every bloody
town
On Thursday night the nation all went out to clap
But the way the government have handled this is just
a pile of crap
Because of the thing called austerity the NHS are
struggling
With the way this government have funded it they
ought to take up juggling
Every day on BBC they pretend they are clarifying
While the key workers on the front line have already
started dying
They don't have protective clothing or the equipment
that they need

The only reason that it's like this is privatised
industry greed
And it's definitely gonna get worse long before it's
better
But don't worry folks cos your government is sending
you a letter
They initiated a lockdown but didn't say it was
mandatory
So thousands flocked to the beaches but that's another
story
Those of you self employed they'll help you out in
June
But that is about as much use now as howling at the
moon
They get on the TV and blah, blah, blah about
slowing the corona threat
But when it's done and dusted you'll owe them
corona debt

So here I am in isolation thinking about this stuff
While the government try to spin another corona bluff

CORONASPIRACIES

Where did it come from what are they doing?
When it's done and dusted will civilisation be lain ruin?
Since before this virus appeared governments had become far seedier
And you'll scare the shirt right off your back believing social media
In the New World Order Coronaspiracies abound
Every day a new one makes our heads spin round
They made it in a laboratory but we know not who they are
The men behind the men behind or something as bizarre
It isn't real it's just a scam is what I hear folks say
But many people don't survive to see another day
It's all 5g I hear some say which makes me quite amused
Another pile of bullshit to make people Coronafused
Civilisation was starting to crumble they were fearful at the top
So the governments got together to make dissension stop
I can't believe the stuff I hear it spins my head around
But in the New World Order Coronaspiracies abound
But there is a really good side effect that isn't all that strange
The air is getting clearer is this Corona Climate Change?
Because the World's is virtually locked down very few planes and cars

And industry almost at a stop and restaurants, cafes and bars
Now many have been encouraged to become a neighbourhood snitch
And every time a car door slams a hundred curtains twitch
Then the governments award themselves another ten grand more
To sit at home like the heroes they are and fight this viral war
While people are literally penniless and food is getting short
Those with an extra ten grand payout can afford more coke to snort
So what could be the answer? I really wish I knew
But there's a one-eyed yellow idol to the north of Kathmandu,
There's a little marble cross below the town;
There's a broken-hearted woman tends the grave of me and you,
And the Yellow God forever gazes down.

WORDS

BY

ALUN BUFFRY

Born in Wales 1950, moved to Norwich 1968, graduated in Chemistry at UEA 1971. Started my travels in 1972, Worked for HMP 1991 to 1995, In 1999, he co-founded the Legalise Cannabis Alliance (LCA), a political party in the UK. Started writing 1997: Books include 'All Abut My Hat The Hippy Trail 1972', "The Prison Years', 'Damage and Humanity in Custody', "Out of Joint 20 Years of Campaigning for Cannabis', 'Myhat in Egypt Through The Eyes of a God', "The Effie Enigma The Motherless Mothers', 'Inside My Hat and Other Heads' with others. Joyful living peace.

http://www.buffry.org.uk/buffry.html

AND THERE I WAS

And There I Was
With no because.
I travelled on, to sing my song,

To soar up high, to seek and try
To find my Self, beyond earthly wealth,
Within inside, the changing tides,
Through cities close and distant lands,
Mountains, rivers, desert sands.
Towards life's end,
My Tale I send,
And here within,
My Tale begins.
For there I was,
With no because.

THE NURSERY

Mary, Mary, quite contrary,
How does your garden grow?
With Widows and Hazes
That doctors amazes,
At pretty buds all in a row.

Little Miss Puffit,
She grew some nice stuff, it
Eases her pains and her Mind,
But along came the law and smashed down he door,
And dragged poor Miss Puffit behind.

Doctor, doctor, an imposter,
Would not prescribe a plant,
Unless one paid the incredible fee.
Now doctor's been humbled,
'cos Guy has been tumbled,
As growing Weed is Free.

HOW MANY TIMES

How many times must a man be afraid of the sound
of a knock on his door?

Yes 'n' how many times must he live in fear of those
who uphold the law?

Yes 'n' how many times must the public pay to take
themselves to the courts?

Yes 'n' how many times must a mother watch her
innocent children caught?

The answer my friends, is blowing in the wind, the
answer is blowing in the wind.

How many families will be split apart when a father is
sent to jail?

Yes 'n' how many times lives must be lost to bad
drugs because of a law that fails?

Yes 'n' how much pain must be felt by a man that
could be eased by a plant?

Yes 'n' how suffering will not be cured because of the
drugs that can't

The answer my friends, is blowing in the wind, the
answer is blowing in the wind.

How many years must be passed while we wait to be free to smoke the good herb?

Yes 'n' how many times must we see the judge before we get the rights we deserve?

Yes 'n' how many drugs must a doctor sell before we can grow our own ease?

Yes 'n' how many drugs must a patient take when cannabis can cure the disease?

The answer my friends, is blowing in the wind, the answer is blowing in the wind.

How many fines must the people pay before they're allowed to get high?

Yes 'n' how many times will a Government hide before they will legalise?

Yes 'n' how many lives will be spoilt by a law when the law is meant to protect?

Yes 'n' how many cells will the prisoners fill for the good of a law that's suspect?

The answer my friends, is blowing in the wind, the answer is blowing in the wind.

THE WORLD THAT IS FOR EVER CHANGING

In this our time the world has changed,
It seems our Lives are re-arranged.
The Tyrants, they have made their laws,
To try to keep us all indoors.

Once we gathered, groups of friends,
Now we think that's reached the end.
Are those laws so right or wrong?
Regardless we must each stay strong.

No more gatherings in the streets,
No more protests bad laws to beat,
Through emails, Twitter, Facebook and Skype,
What we once shouted now we must type.

I thought this world was meant for me.
I thought mankind should all be free.
To travel roads and seas and skies,
To Live our Lives so we feel high.

Right now the virus makes some fright.
Governments tell us alone is Right.
Inside our homes they want us to hide,
Yet happiness and joy remains inside.

This time must pass as all time does.
What we must keep is peace and love.
Bad laws we know they'll introduce,
Our peaceful conformity to seduce.

But look at it another way.
Don't let our hearts to hatred sway.
For life is not just about this world,
our lives inside us always unfurled.

What's still important for you and me,
is what lies inside that each must see.
Whatever happens in our lives,
For peace and love we each must strive

BUMBLING BORIS

Bumbling Boris make no sense,
The red virus outside your fence,
But you can walk now, mile on mile,
Wear a face mask, don't show your smile.

You can be outside all the day,
Go to work and earn your pay,
Sit inside your local park,
They'll be unlocked 'til it gets dark.

Play your sports with family,
Run your life but alert please be,
You'll be fined if you break the rules,
Soon the infants back to schools.

Keep your distance, stay apart,
Fill your wheelie shopping cart,
Use your plastic bankers cards,
Spare the beds on hospital wards.

Control the virus when it's red,
Keep the colours in your head,
Ease the lockdown, ease it slow,
Bumbling Boris doesn't know.

LEADING CLOWNS

You may well think our leaders clowns,
For sure they let the people down.
It matters not were you come from,
If your name's Boris Jacob of Dom.

Unless you're in the Upper Class,
Workers will stay upon their ass.
It matters more where they went to school.
Eaton and Oxford were so cool.

They had a grand old party time,
That's why they pull the Party line.
They laugh and tell us what to do,
Won't listen to the likes of You.

We vote and think our votes will count,
Lead us to what we think we want,
We praise them for the little they give,
They hide away the way they live.

And when they want to fight a war,
They ask all all to give some more.
They sale their yachts and ride their horses,
They play with their balls on their golf courses.

They drink their champers and fine wines,
They eat their gourmet meals so fine,
Put chemicals in our food and water,
Send our soldiers out for slaughter.

Yet deep inside we're all the same,
It matters not your family name,
For when we each the end of life,
It's them that will suffer the strife.

It's them that will see they're bad,
it's them in loneliness will fee sad,
It's them that did us all that bad,
It's them that last breath will be so sad.

For one thing to them I'd like to teach,
That in this life we each need peace.
It's not in glory, wealth or fame.
It's only in our Soul's true name.

THE DART BOARD OF JOY

Life (your life) is like a dart board when all you need to do to get everything that you truly need and desire will be yours if you can just hit the board with a dart.

You don't even need to hit the bull or double top; you don't need to hit a number; you just need to hit the board.

If only you had a dart!

What does each of us truly need and desire? What is at the end of every want?

Peace, love, joy, clarity, understanding, freedom, appreciation, satisfaction, contentment, fulfilment, call it whatever but it is the same. That is what makes us strive for things in this world- for things that will make, or at least we hope they will make, us feel good.

If only we had a dart.

Then, for me, along came a man who told me he knew that I did have dart, but I had forgotten where it was and he could show me where it was. His name is Prem Rawat and since that day when he did show me, I have tried to explain this to others who so often seem so desperate.

That was almost 50 years ago and he has constantly reminded me where to look to find that dart that has been inside me all the time and that I believe is inside every person that is human.

So, pretty unbelievably simply? Just get the dart and throw it as the board. Even if I miss sometimes, I need to keep trying – and practice makes perfect. And it is free, no charge, no committent other than to myself to keep practising.

I have seen other people who just don't believe me. That's OK, just carry on looking for peace and joy that will be everywhere with you.

I have seen people that found the dart but never throw it at the board. That's OK, at least they found the dart and know where it is if they ever want to try throwing it.

I have seen people just throw it over their shoulder. That's OK, they can pick it up some time and try throwing it at the board and if they miss, just pick it up and try again.

I have seen people just throw it away. That's OK because it will stay where they threw it – nobody else can take or use that dart, it is theirs.

And I have seen people that threw it at the board and

every time they miss, they try again and every time they hot the board it is so good for them as it has been for me.

I have seen people just like myself that sometimes forget all about the dart and the board and get carried away with distractions that are all around, like adverts, falsely offering lasting joy and peace. That's OK because Prem Rawat comes along and reminds me.

It really has been and remains such an important Knowledge in my life that I really want to say to everybody just give it a try. If you like it, fine; if you don't like it, but that is just fine too.

Prem Rawat will be offering access to his Peace Education Programme (PEP) on-line to everyone.

I hope that YOU will give it a try.

http://www.premrawat.com

ON THE HEAD OF AMENY

Taken from
Myhat in Egypt Through the Eyes of a God
by Alun Buffry

A few days later, I had the biggest surprise of life time since I first met Ed.

Suddenly, after playing hoops, Ameny asked Ed if he could try me on and if it would be agreeable with Ed to make a similar hat for himself, in the colours white and red, signifying Upper and Lower Egypt.

Ed knew that the white crown of Upper Egypt was officially known as the Hedjet, whilst the Red Crown of Lower Egypt was called the Deshret. After Egypt had been unified, the double crown, red and white, was called the Pschent. That was several hundred years before Ameny and the double crown would be worn by him when he became Pharaoh, as it was by his father Senwosret.

Ed was not in the habit of letting others wear me, although I had been on Ana's head and a few others over the years. He could hardly say no to a boy god who was his host, so he took me off, bowed and presented me to Ameny.

What a revelation!

The boy totally believed that he was of divine birth, that he was a god and that he was all powerful. Only his own father was above him in rank.

I realised that that Ameny regarded everyone else as inferior, including Ed and Ana, other members of his own family and court, including the many Priests that he regarded with suspicion and as struggling to gain position in his eyes.

He had little genuine respect or care for anyone, not even his own family and, as Ameny knew his successors had done, was quite prepared to destroy people's lives and use people for his own purposes.

Ameny knew that one day he may have to dispose of his father. He felt that when he openly worshipped the gods, he was worshipping only what he was.

Ana's name meant Goddess. Ameny knew that Ed and Ana came to him from a very far away and mysterious place, a place where huge birds carried people through the skies and people communicated through the air even showing pictures through their mysterious boxes powered by an unseen energy called electricity which was, he had concluded, a great gift from the gods.

Ameny saw himself as indestructible: he could do whatever he wanted to or with whoever he wanted, except he could not fly.

The head of Ameny was nothing like the head of Ed, or Ana, or any other head that I been upon. The world view was so different that I became almost lost in it.

For the first time in my existence, I understood that it was I that was the superior being. I had a better memory and better understanding of many things than Ed. If I was to remain on the head of Ameny, I could rule the world.

CONNECT 2121

Taken from
The Effie Enigma, The Motherless Mothers

by

Alun Buffry

Agent ZX (Zedex) had mixed feelings about being called to the Connect HQ. On the one hand, it meant endless hours scanning through news reports, watching old news films and scratching away at connections. On the more positive side, an opportunity to meet his latest crush, Agent QT, whom he called Cutie, from the Far East Sector of Connect. They had communicated virtually several times, but the thought of meeting Cutie in the flesh gave him goose pimples.

In the old days they used to call this day Saint Valentines Day.

But, thought Zedex, what chance do I have? Cutie is an attractive young man, just about 22 years of age, with olive skin, visible muscles and long blond hair. Zedex himself was probably, he thought, more of a father figure than a potential flesh-on-flesh lover. Now 98-years-old, rotund, balding, he still wore the old-fashion spectacles. He had never been comfortable with instant vision surgery that most had received. All they had in common was that they were both investigating Crisis Connections and had both previously been with the military. Anyway, current events that were bringing them together was serious and they would have to focus.

But, remembered Zedex, Cutie will only have seen perfected image projection of him and vice versa. To Cutie, Zedex would have appeared forty years younger, several kilos lighter and with a full head of hair. And Zedex knew nothing about how Cutie actually looked in the flesh. This first meeting could well be a make-or-break.

Earlier that day, Zedex had been called to the HQ after four more deaths, this time all scientists all connected with Project Outreach. At the same time, there had been a failed attempt on the life of Professor John Sullivan, the creator of the portable wormhole in time. Certainly this leaned towards the conspiracy theory.

So Zedex had taken an auto-hover car which enabled him to quickly catch up with the paperwork. Nowadays, few people moved about the city other than in auto-hovers which were remarkably safe. Fewer people actually travelled about the city than previously. What with food parcels delivered to your door, virtual teaching through the PLATO programme, the Planetary Tuition Optimisation scheme that brought almost identical tuition schedules into almost every home and put an end to the "school run" traffic chaos that Zedex had grown up with.

Zedex had received his instructions and a minimum amount of information via his retinal-link. Despite the safety record of auto-hovers, all four scientists, two men and two women, had died as a result of hover-car accidents. The chances of that being simple coincidence was indeed slim.

Connect was officially established way back in 2021, two years even before Zedex had been born (of course he was not called ZX back then) to investigate apparent connections between various historical events seriously retarding progress on Project Outreach, the building of the A.I.-controlled Mother-ships that would eventually enable distant planets to become human colonies, literally billions of years and even light-years from Earth. A.I. and robotics, cryogenics and space exploration itself were progressing comfortably but these events, whether connected or not, were slowing the project down to the point where earth's own problems could bring a halt to the project completely.

Zedex had entered Connect in 2098 and had been working virtually with Cutie for several years now and had listed incidents that had caused the delays in or seemed to have tried to delay project Outreach.
Until now it had appeared that it was merely a conspiracy theory that there existed a well-hidden

long-term project to delay or stop Outreach. It had not officially been taken very seriously and Zedex's work was hardly a workload

It was only now, with the sudden death of four essential scientists, that the newly appointed World President had prioritised the Connect project. The recent discovery of how humans and possibly others could use portable wormholes and the possibility of travelling through time introduced an entirely new line of investigation. It may become possible for people to travel to the past and make dangerous changes, cause all sorts of paradoxes; or even to the future. The possible assassination of the man that had become the leading edge in that technology, Professor John Sullivan, increased the likelihood that there was a connection between assassins over the decades and now there was news that Sullivan's suspected assassin had been "examined" and apparently the assassin thought he was indeed from the future and on a mission.

ZX sketched by Jacqui Malkin

Photos by Alun Buffry

A POEM

BY

MELISSA DOORDAUGHTER

Melissa is a teacher who lives in a village in Northern Italy with her husband and two children. She graduated in Anthropology and Religion at the University of Wales and took up teaching. She has written several small books – 'For Precise Reason' and 'Fragments of Her Story' and had several poems and stories included in 'Inside My Hat and Other Heads'

COLLECTING COINS

When I was seventeen, I had a dream
I was one of the Chosen Ones.
But now I see that it isn't me.
Oh no, no, no, not at all.
The waves of time have taken
My self security, that religious egotism
And swept it out to sea.
What remains is a beggar
Trying to swim against the tide,
Collecting coins of righteousness.
And a thorn stuck in her side,
The crumbs and scraps of memories
Were once a mantel of gold,
But now, alas, faded and torn.,
And I am getting old.
Maybe there is sanctuary in the garden.
I will search for a different joy,
A Cloak of magnolia petal,
To relinquish easily.

WORDS
by
MARS BILTERS

The little known Yorkshire poet Mars Bilters is a prolific writer of herb verse, and an advocate and lover of cannabis. Mars finds THC to be an effective analgesic for his knee that he's broke 3 times. He lived and worked in Spain as a gardener amongst other things. He studied at Hull University and Córdoba. Mars also finds cannabis to be a spiritual facilitator and sacrament, enhancing body, soul and mind, and also a key to mystical awareness and intuition. Mars likes nothing better than to sit beneath a tree and imbibe a chalice or 3, so he may contemplate the meaning of life and how to give meaning to his life.

https://tembilofhashlam.co.uk

HOME GROWN CANNABIS
AN INALIENABLE ACT

Personal cannabis cultivation is harmless
Cannabis plants are not a threat to society
Indoor ganjah gardens are not a menace
To grow herbs at home is a private matter
A plant is a plant whether hemp or pepper
A tomato, potato, cauliflower or cannabis
They all have the status of nutritional food
All have the potential to benefit our bodies
What we grow in our veg patch is our affair
The state has no business in folks gardens
The govs ideological cannabis war is bogus
A law against cannabis does not have merit
Pot edicts do not have honour and are unjust
This archaic herb ban doesn't have consent
It was initiated by greedy ill informed tyrants
Men long dead made hemp illegal for profits
Time has come to reverse the trend and grow
Grow on a windowsill, allotment or herb beds
Build a grow room utilising health and safety
The privacy of a person's home is sacrosanct
Intrusion by state is an indignation and tyranny
To enter homes by force to pull up pot flowers
Is an abuse of power, an act of state violence
And a huge waste of police time and resource
All to stop a harmless beneficial plant growing
What we grows in our homes is our prerogative
Personal herb cultivation is our harmless hobby
Our hobby should be left alone so we can thrive
Allowed to home grow healing crops in privacy

GROW YOUR OWN CANNABIS PLANTS

A substance of mercy delivers great relief
Natural compassion found in ganja leafs
The mercy of cannabis is grown with love
A gardening therapy of sweet healing buds
A home-grown remedy of potent efficiency
A vital supplement to end canna deficiency
Hemp an analgesic used since olden times
Healer of broke bodies, a soother of minds
Oil of cannabis is most beneficial and kind
THC and CBD to our receptors they do bind
Symbiotic link to endocannabinoid system
Merciful sticky flowers grow tall on a stem
Humanity is divinely connected to cannabis
We need pot to live and thrive or we get sick
Herb vital as a food, a seed of amino acids
Cannabis makes annoying numbness placid
Eases throbbing limbs and irritating spasms
Delivers folk serenity, out of a painful chasm
To grow plants at home for a medicinal need
Harms no one, isn't a threat nor an evil deed
Home grown plants can deliver sweet mercy
Pot shouldn't be persecuted or a controversy
Plants of mercy police shouldn't ever disturb
So enshrine our right to grow our own herbs

THE TREE OF LOVE
A BLESSING TO HUMANITY

The lovers of Cannabis Sativa are growing
Every day more folks partake in cannabis
Pot attitudes and opinions have changed
People are better educated about ganja
Better informed about the cannabis plant
Herb truth once suppressed is now known
It's common knowledge buds are healthy
Herb is imperative to end THC deficiency
THC and CBD both vital to all our well-being
A daily endocannabinoid system necessity
The adherents of sticky flowers are agreed
Hashish oil is holy, holistic and wholesome
It's the best substances there is for Wo/men
A green sacrament for body, mind and soul
A peaceful relaxant full of positive creativity
An organic elixir of many subtle benefits
The aficionados of the grass of giggles grow
Casting seeds and cultivating without fears
For the love of cannabis plants many do toil
The lovers of Cannabis Sativa are everywhere
They are informed, well researched and eager
To share their experiences and cannabis info
And spread cannabis knowledge to everyone
For everyone has an endocannabinoid system
Every man, woman and child is a cannabis tree

HER UNLAWFUL PAINFUL
CANNABIS PLIGHT

She just wants to medicate naturally
To feel the benefits of cannabis oils
To ease her pain and stop her tremors
So she can get a good night of sleepin'
To feel refreshed and rested on weed
So she doesn't feel nauseous or groggy
Her appetite is nearly back to normality
Her mood lifted, her depression is eased
She just wants to feel cannabis benefits
Without fear of arrest nor prison threats
She doesn't want to worry about police
She just wants to rapidly ease her pains
Without having to look over her shoulder
Or anxiety about kicking in her front door
She is just a quiet lady in desperate pain
And at times her bad aching is unbearable
She's no choice but to administrate herb
She's past caring about unlawful claims
Ready to face any unlawful consequence
Her life, health and sanity depend on herb
She ignores corrupt and evil cannabis edict
Her use of herb is a true medical necessity
Her need for weed is above man made law
The law's an ass as God created CANNABIS!

SAT SMOKIN'
BENEATH A CRESCENT MOON

He smokes all night sebsi after sebsi
From sunset 'til the new sun does rise
Pot fume reddens his bloodshot eyes
Bowl after bowl of long stemmed pipe
Smoking all night much to his delight
It be the ninth lunar month of ramazan
He broke fast with soup and hashish
Now he be at peace with holy El Khadir
Lucidly dreamy and languidly thinking
He feels chilled and mystically stoned
Contemplating the enigma of existence
The metaphysical nature of everything
And the meaning of his mad chaotic life
Until the sun rises he sits with his sebsi
Imbibing the golden fume of relaxation
When the sun rises he'll stop his toking
He'll put down his pipe until the evening
Then once more hash fume he'll breathe
And set to stoned contemplation again

WORDS
by
RYAN KIEF

Around 6 years ago, when I was in my mid twenties, I was given an auto-immune condition, ankylosing spondylitis. It came with its usual traits, pain brought on by inflammation, fatigue and joint stiffness causing mobility issues. It stopped me on my tracks in a promising music career. I was a DJ and a salesman for a DJ company so I was working six or seven days and nights most weeks. It took a toll on my health and the medication I was prescribed had many negative effects. I then began to research cannabis and a new journey began.

https://helpmehemp.uk/
https://www.facebook.com/groups/helpmehemp

FREEDOM

Together we will grow.
Forever we will support.
Wherever, we will go
To show up in court.

Our lives are dedicated
To keep each other medicated
But our freedom is our crime
And for this we donate our time.

When will this plant be free?
Why won't the governments see?
That this natural plant
Is here for you and me.

GROW

Grow, grow, grow your plant
Germinate the seed
If the law tells you no!
Tell them it's what we need.

BUD

I'm a little weed bud
Crisp and tight
Help you with your problems
I just might.
When things get too much
And life wants wants to fight
Just roll me up
And set me alight.

SEED

Tiny, tiny little seed
How do you give me what I need?
Of all the plants in this word,
It is your powers that they have dispelled.
Tiny, tiny little seed
We need to grow you and be freed.

STOLE

How can you be so cruel
And treat us like a fool.
For thousands of years you have tried denying,
That the powers of the plant are multiplying.
From anxiety to arthritis,
With meds you prescribe us
But you insist that the plant brings no relief
And stole it from us like a thief.

LEGALISATION

Why am I so hated?
My legalisation highly anticipated.
Are you with me or against me?
The people who suffer,
They need to be free.
The earth is for us to share
And you have ripped me from it,
Without a care.
For you humans I have so much to give.
Just let me be free and allow you to live.

TEACH

You can call me marijuana or even Mary Jane
Whatever you know me as I am here for your pain
Turn away from what they try to teach
Do your own research and then you can preach
the benefits of cultivating me for human
consumption.
Without my powerful goodness your system does not
function.
The flowers I produce are indeed for human use
Whether you want me for my CBD or THC
I produce them all for humans you see.

VIRUS

Whilst the earth stood still,

Mother nature began to heal.

Years after the industrial revolution,

Humans causing too much pollution.

She began to choke

With floods and fires she tried warning folk

But we gave her no resolution

Everyone told to stay at home,

Whilst mother nature reclaims her throne.

Shops not essential began to close,

Streets and cities where time had froze.

The pollution levels began to fall,

With an economy that once stood tall.

Our luxuries and wants we now don't need,

This is a time that we can be freed.

We may have fear in our mind,

But look deeper and you will find.

This virus, a threat to humanity,

But through this we will find clarity.

A new world order which we must abide,

Lets be human again, let's not hide.

We are one, living together.

Hurt her again we must never.

LEGS

I miss walking in the fresh air,
I miss jogging around the field without a care.
I miss playing music every weekend
I miss going to the pub with a friend.
My legs, they used to work you see
Now I no longer can be free.

Free to walk down the stairs,
Free to jog around that field with no cares.
Free to lay on the fresh cut green,
Free to be free again like my teens.
My legs, they used to work you see
Now I no longer can be free.

Photos by Alun Buffry

WORDS
by
SARAH DOUGAN AKA SARAH SATIVA

I live in Spain and run a Cannabis Club called Shamballa CSC in Quesada. I've worked with and grown cannabis since 2003 but consumed it since around 1994. I love it and my live revolves around this beautiful plant which has so much to offer us and the planet. I started being an advocate back in 2013 after doing radio shows with Rick Simpson, since then I have not looked back at all. I've helped and guided 1000's through their journey of consuming cannabis for medicinal reasons and how to grow. love writing poems and have been witting them since 2013

I have my own CBD company Sarah Sativa CBD which I love and look forward to the day I can add THC products to this in the UK and other countries. I've seen this planet improve people's and give them hope where there once was none.

I run pages on Facebook and on Instagram Sarah Sativa, SarahSativa CBD and Shamballa CSC. I also have two websites for information and guidance of consuming cannabis medicinally.

www.sarahsativa.com
www.sarahsativacbd.com

113

NEW WAY OF BEING

To take those steps that lead to a new life
Can at first seem like an impossible journey,
So daunting
And so far away.
A million and one excuses and reasons can pop into
your head
As why not take those steps.
The more you put it off the harder and further away it
feels
When you realise by moving your focus on now,
On what you can do,
No matter how small,
The dream can become a reality.
It doesn't mean you won't feel scared.
It doesn't mean you won't pause or take a bit of a step
back.
What it does mean with every minute, every day you
do focus, that dream becomes more of a reality.
The vulnerability is part of a new existence,
A new way of being.
It's there to move through and shine even brighter.
Live this life; you have the best possible way.
Be kind, show love, be honest.
Let go of limitations,
Negative patterns,
Believing in lack.

ASSUMPTIONS AND EXPECTATIONS

I don't know,
So I will assume
My mate doesn't like you
So I don't either.
I expect this and that.
You don't give it.
That makes you a twat.
Answer me now,
Not when you have time.
My expectations
Must be met.
My assumptions
Are correct.
You owe me this
'Cause I did that.
That's why I hate you.
That's why I get my mates to join in.
Oh the drama!
Oh the lies!
Keeps our focus,
From what's real,
From what's true,
From really seeing.
How you behave?
Who you really our?
Slander here, slander there,
Everyone's heads spinning.
So much shit,
Most of it made up.

Why can't we put our differences aside?
Look at our own behaviour!
Never mind your neighbours!
One 💝 love,
One world,
All connected intertwined.
What you give you get.
What you focus on you become.
Get real!
Get love!

WHEN YOU LOOK IN THE MIRROR
WHAT DO YOU SEE?

When you look in the mirror what do you see?
Can you look into your eyes and say I see love?
When you are sat on your own,
How do you feel?
Can you sit in silence?
Can you sit in peace?
Or do you have to keep moving?
Do you put your focus on others and how bad you
make them out to be?
I know me,
I've spent time sat on my own,
I can sit in peace,
I can see the love in my eyes,
And feel it in my heart.
Can you or are you so scare?
Cause you know you are a cunt?

THERE IS ENOUGH OF EVERYTHING
TO GO ROUND

We live in a society
Where we compete with each other,
Where we break each other down to get further,
Where the shy and timid are ridiculed and bullied,

It's a society where the loudest and most dominant
are mostly heard,
Where they fight for control,
Control of others,
Control of situations,

It's like it's sculpting people to compete,

TO BE HARD

I'm a bit of a hippy myself.
I see what a difference building each other up does.
I'm not here to compete with others.
I'm not here to laugh at others.
I'm not here to break people.

People spend so much time,
Focused on others,
Focused on what others don't have,

Rather than what they have,
Their own unique beauty,
Copying each other rather then working with each
other,

There is enough of everything to go round.
The world is a full-on place for real people.

Have a blessed day

LA LA LAND

La La Land
Is where most people live.

La La land
Is that safe place.
That safe place where you don't have to do anything,

La La Land
Is where you convince yourself its all alright

La La Land,
Where you can watch people be battered,
Where you can watch people get hurt
And do nothing 'cause.

La La Land
Is that safe place
Where you convince yourself its OK to stand by
And do nothing.

La La Land,
Where its OK to do nothing.

I bet you don't want to be woken up from
Your La La Land,
That nice safe place where you don't have to do
anything.

La La Land,
That nice safe place
Where
BANG YOU ARE NOW FUCKED!
YOU ARE NOW IN REALITY

It's hit you like a ton of bricks.
Oh yeah, you really did stand by and do nothing.

Yes the world is a fucked-up place!
But its better than
La La Land,
That nice safe place where you cant hide for ever.

Photos by Alun Buffry

WORDS

By

PHIL MONK

Phil Monk is a father of 3, once teacher of adult literacy, numeracy, Spanish and ESOL, now blighted by long-term disability from chronic myofascial pain from joint hypermobility spectrum disorder, bilateral ulnar impaction syndrome, arthritis, PTSD and depression.

Four life-threatening hospitalisations after taking prescribed pharmaceutical drugs and the government refusing to recognise the therapeutic benefits of cannabis, resulted in Phil becoming campaigner and founder of "We The Undersigned Have a Human Sovereign Right to Cannabis" (WTU)

Phil says "The War on Cannabis, is really a war on cannabis consumers and our preferred way of life, and has lead me to believe that cannabis is food before medicine or recreational drug and everyone should have the right to grow it for whatever purpose they choose, free from the fear of prosecution. **http://www.wtuhq.org/**

GENERAL ELECTION 2019
PROPORTIONAL REPRESENTATION
PETITION

The General Election was painful to watch
So many fooled by media botch
More misinformation and false promise
State sanctioned lying is plainly remiss
So many friends and family broken
All down to many lies that were spoken
So many friends drawing lines in the sand
General Election division goes hand in hand
Divide, conquer and rule the masses
Our country is run by a House of Asses
One racist bigot lying with impunity
The other good name slurred by media community
The irony is that many believe
Our election system doesn't deceive
That the system it true and fair
Yet voters apathy causes despair
When a majority rule on minority vote
So the wealthy elite can claim for their moat
The latest result causing much consternation
To undemocratic disproportionate representation
This biased two horse race
Really becomes a slap in the face
With many voting tactically
And definitely not ideologically
Some even wonder if all is pre ordained
The media circus leaving families pained
From lies and deceit leaving them all drained
The British political system is truly stained

But some have made it their mission
To make fairer election decision
And have launched meaningful petition
For fairer proportional representation
Although I somewhat doubt
That those with all the clout
Will acquiesce to such request
Even though at public behest
For if they granted such a wish
They'd be out of water like landed fish
For if they granted true and fair proportional powers
It would knock them from their Ivory Towers
Even so I have signed and shared
In the hope more will be prepared
To make a stand against this mimicry
And the Great British Demockeracy!

WAKE UP CALL

Early hours
Suddenly
Wide awake
Gasping breath
Treacle brain
Foggy mind
Eyes open
Through closed lids
Muscles spasmed
Iron tight
Fist clenched up
Pincky pains
Toes all curled
Shins aching
Hips hurting
Guts churning
Bladder full
Standing rock
Spine seized tight
Shoulders locked
Feeling like
Living corpse
Waking From
Rigors Mort
Dreadful pain
For day's start

Immobile
Blessed be
Mary Jane
Easing aches
Dead Chem Head
A real treat
Vaped flower
Spasms melt
Herb Power.

EASING MY PAINS

Every day
Waking the same
Another Groundhog
Day of pain
Limbs painful, heavy and stiff
Time to light me a big phat spliff
I don't smoke to get high,
No matter how hard I try
I smoke to get by
To lift my mind
From the mud
To ease aching muscles
And swollen joints.
Some may say
Its smell offends
But hardly worth prison
I would defend
It not only eases my pain
But elevates my mind
That I don't enjoy it
I won't pretend
Best method yet
To manage my health
Made criminal by
Government stealth
Who misled our Nation
For personal wealth
Denied therapeutic benefits
Of traditional herbal remedy

While making monopolies
And high profits
With decades of lies
Prosecuted millions
Destroyed countless lives
Of those who choose
Fragrant flowers of Cannabis
Sometimes instead of booze
Sometimes pharmaceuticals
Seeking their own personal bliss
Should this choice make one lose
Your home, family or freedom
Because you got high
And didn't get
Pissed?
The freedom of consciousness
They barely miss

WHO KNOWS?

What is what?
And what is not?
Simple truth
We simply haven't got.
Altogether I don't trust
The Powers that Be.
Completely over our lives
They wish to foresee
For care or for profit
Time will reveal
Just how much was
For the people's health
Or Political zeal
Or corporate stealth
With primary motives
To increase their wealth
Control our lives
Behind our backs
Sinister forces contrive
Friends and family
Breaking apart
No one knows
what's fact or fiction
Such is the level
Of misinformation
As we have been fed lies
from the start
So far from truth
The government depart.
Causing much fear

And deliberation
Resulting in fall outs
And social division.
When now is time
For community clout.
To rally together
In time of need
Whilst keeping
Your distance
At Government heed.
Meanwhile I remain
At home
Keeping in contact
Through my phone
Until signs of safety
Return.
Keep well my friends
And your spirits high
Don't give up the fight
Nor resign to sigh
If we're lucky
Perhaps the end is nigh
And usual life will resume.
Keep well in the meantime

Love, light and peace

CANNABIS CURE vs PREVENTION

I don't see cannabis as a cure or medicine, in my own humble yet reasonably informed opinion.

From what I have read I have concluded that Cannabis is food before medicine and only appears medicinal in nature when reintroduced to a deficient and malfunctioning endocannabinoid system, which manifests as disease or illness.

I do believe from what I have learned that cannabis maintains and regulates homeostasis

The closer our bodies are to homeostasis the better our health and well-being.

So I believe that when cannabis is introduced to a prohibition induced endocannabinoid deficient system, that manifests as disease, the entourage of phytocannabinoids nourish and replenish the depleted endocannabinoid system, thereby returning to, or as close as possible as the damaged physiology is able, to homeostasis.

Sometimes that could be an improvement in the symptoms of disease/deficiency, management of symptoms or reversal completely and a full return to homeostasis, health and well-being.

I suspect that depending on the severity of the endocannabinoid deficiency it would likely determine how close the return to homeostasis can be.

Some barely, some partially and some completely, I anticipate.

Cannabis is a remarkably nutritious herb and I would argue is an essential nutrient in the maintenance of health.

I would further argue that the many modern diseases that blight our lives are a result of the fraudulent prohibition of phytocannabinoids from the human diet and food chain completely.

I would further ponder whether the continued enforcement of said prohibition would not result in a generational genetic devolution of the endocannabinoid system, resulting in poor homeostasis from significantly earlier ages, manifesting as diseases; especially in view of the generally deteriorating nutritional value of what many now consume as food yet has virtually no true nutritional value.

Whereas, if cannabis were ubiquitously available and consumed as food in its entirety for all its incredible potential nutritional value and full entourage of phytocannabinoids, all would have access to that which would regulate and maintain homeostasis in their bodies, through the cannabis interacting then regulating their endocannabinoid system, which could only improve health and well-being, thereby potentially reducing the incidence of disease, depending upon other lifestyle factors of course.

I could present many papers to support all of my thoughts and beliefs while an equally dedicated person could also present papers to support their beliefs that cannabis is a harmful schedule 1 drug that causes addiction and psychosis.

I guess my point is that there is so much propaganda and misinformation as well as quality research it can make it very difficult to discern which is fact and which is prohibitionist fiction.

My final point is that WTU fight for the freedom of beliefs and practices for all.

So if someone believes that cannabis can cure all, then who I am I to judge them or tell them otherwise?

For I know not what they know nor have read nor learned what they have.

So even if if doesn't align with my own beliefs it does not mean to say they are wrong to hold their beliefs or me to hold mine.

To each their own.

No one has responsibility for the actions of another, only their own.

I think it is the complete responsibility of each individual to perform their own research and learning to inform themselves fully before making any decisions on any matter.

Whether through sharing personal experiences or through academic research or whatever means as much information can be found from each other too.

Cannabis cures all, well evidently not as many can confirm cannabis hasn't cured them, myself included.

Maybe if I had not been deprived of cannabis as nutrition maybe I would not be crippled by chronic myofascial pain from joint hypermobility spectrum disorder and arthritis?

Maybe these conditions are down to my mercury fillings or even childhood vaccinations, poor diet, a hereditary disease or just poor dumb luck.

Maybe if I were able to consume adequate concentrated cannabis as food I may return to homeostasis?
But just maybe cannabis as food to balance homeostasis could prevent all?
If part of a healthy lifestyle especially that is.

Who knows....

ISOLATION

During this period of 'pandemic'
Important not to give in to panic
When so many theories abound
One of them, eventually,
Has to be sound.
Is this natural disaster
Created by Nature's Master?
Or, even more absurd,
Man-made virus to thin the herd?
Is this all a deep state cover up
Of the global rollout of killer 5G?
Many seem to think something's up
I guess we'll have to wait and see.
If not for their lies and deception
That since 2014 I did find
Many beyond comprehension
That well and truly blew my mind
I would believe the official story
Not even have a shadow of doubt
Bow down to their power and glory
Instead now my gut gives doubtful shout
The Political, Corporate and Media Class
For decades have tricked and lied
Destroying billions of lives of working brass
For profit and control they've decried
That cannabis is truly a healing herb
Which Improves health and many ailments
Quite contrary to government blurb
It's possessors not worthy of imprisonment

FORMER SELF ON THE SHELF

As I sit here former shadow of myself
Trapped in my house, left on the shelf
No care nor treatment proffered
Just nasty addictive drugs offered
To manage the pain that destroyed my dreams
Making life unbearable, or so it seems
But my mantra's to keep on smiling, it'll be OK
Despite waking in such pain and dismay
Living in fear of bust and police attack
But learning the truth, I can't turn back
Which catalysed me to years of campaign
Just for the freedom to manage my pain
And for all others to have rights to do the same
We're now trapped by corrupt political game.
The Political Class really ought hang their heads in shame.
Monumental suffering for which they are to blame.

I'M NO POET!

I have never claimed to be a poet
But have often found myself inspired
To express my ideas, fears or joys
Sometimes with rhythm
Or sometimes with rhyme
All I know is from time to time
After a joint instead of glass of wine
Thoughts and ideas start to flow
Then before long
What d'ya know
I've written a poem
That could be a song.
So it's reassuring to learn
Others also find cannabis
Leads them to write
In their inspired bliss.

FEAR AND LIES

Living in fear
Of violent police bust
Of the big red hammer's
Smashing thrust
Waiting anxiously
As passing siren wails
Are they coming for me?
My body quails.
Despite all this
My smile persists
Though my body resists
Screaming joints
With every motion
Always dreading
Violent commotion
Yet I keep on moving
As needs must
I smile to keep
My anandamide flowing
To cope with living
In fear of police bust.
The pen is my sword
And paper my shield
It is all that I am
Just able to wield
Raising awareness
To truths long known
By parliamentarians
Serving the crown
What's that you say,

"Don't they serve us?"
Sad fact is
They'd chuck us
Under a bus
Just to earn
A quick buck
For they simply
Do not
Give
A
Fuck.
They would come
Smash your door in
Ransack your home
With such a din
Searching for
Forbidden fragrant flowers
Alleging they hold
Some sinister powers
To corrupt our soul
And poison our mind
But with due diligence
They would find
That cannabis isn't
Such dangerous drug
We've all been had
By parliamentary thugs
Cannabis is in fact
Nutritious herb

So Please don't fall
For government blurb

Cannabis in fact
Maintains homeostasis
Improving life
Like desert oasis
Millions of lives
Destroyed by lies
All so they can profit
And monopolise
Cannabis is harmful
They preach
Yet they continue
To fail to teach
Aside for 1/4000
That may get psychosis
It's more often red eye
Not quite myxomatosis
Cannabis is safer
Than sugar or booze
It might make you smile
Or even snooze
Nothing however
Is risk free
Go in low and slow
No one's saying
Get out of your tree
Do not drive
When impaired

If you take too much
Don't be too scared
If you feel a bit flighty
In old school terms

It's likely a whitey
Truly not all that different
To getting pissed
But you don't often wake
Wondering what you've missed
No bad guts or brain cells blown
Wondering who you've kissed
Or where your dinners thrown
Instead often there's
Deep contemplation
Of the world's problems
How to save us from damnation
So please don't fall for the propaganda
It's out right lies or herbal slander
Do some research and take a gander
Well known benefits of some proper ganja

Shaun O'Connor response:
My response to which is this; Call this plant the
Healing bloom,
And revel in its gift of bliss,
Not to mention, never killed,
Now the truth is drawing near,
And all will know of natures gifts,
Because the right is ours,

Illegally it has been too long.
Simply, just because.
Welcome it with open arms,
Exalt in natures gift to man.
Ever mindfully of its power.
Due respect is all the flower asks,
People! do not fear the plant,

Or shudder at its name,
Take a closer look.
Someone had a bad idea.
Kill the plant, said Anslinger,
Unfortunately for that misguided man.
Not everyone agreed.
Know the plant, and know your roots, for nature has a
Gift for all.
Dismiss all propaganda,
And the lies, deceit and hypocrisy,
Because combined as one, they cause injustices
Untold.

Janette JJ Clements response:
Do what they will
I will never take a pill
When I can have a lovely plant
On my window sill

Heidi Thompson responded:
I grew mine on the windowsill.
Day by day I watched them grow

143

And remembered the first leaf as it began to show.
Stealthy & healthy it was ready to bloom till them old
Bastards stole her away.

They wrenched her and pulled her right out of her
home only to be told your never going home.
I braved my soul, but the show must go on.
Pills are for deals & weed is for real

Colin Craig response:
This is why I fight this fight,
Because I believe that it is right,

For anyone to have a toke,
It is the laws that are a joke,
The hearts & lives & families broken,
All over what someone was smoking,
More understanding is required,
Before our lives have expired,
So as a family we all celebrate,
All those on here I see as mates,
Can grow our own and share freely,
With social friend or stranger needy,
Without the stress or worry that a harmless act,
Could cause more harm than if you listen to the doc.
We the undersigned are united in our fight for
Freedom for cannabis

SMILE THROUGH PAIN

Waking up
every day
stiff with pain
surprised not
to be busted
yet again.
happy to still
be alive
despite all
the crappy
bits of life.
I would say
the good bits
make it all
worth while,
so I choose
to greet
each day
with a smile.

HAVING A REST

Putting feet up having a rest
A struggle to do even though best
It feels good to do nothing for a day
Thinking of letters and things to say
Binging on Netflix
Instead of going to the Pics
Three-bean chilli in the slow-cooker
Thanks to my son, me ol' mucker
Electric blanket finally easing the aches
Wishing I'd managed to bake some cakes
Feeling grateful for life's sweet mercy
Getting ready to roll with fragrant percy
Hope you're all having a restful day
Ready for next week come what may

APATHY

Apathy seems our most powerful foe...
And, as ever Alun Buffry, you're in the know...
Imagine if all who pledge support became active
campaigners instead of passive supporter....
Then maybe the government wouldn't beat us like
we're lambs to the slaughter?
50 years fighting for truth, justice and freedom
To have the right to sow cannabis seeds in our own
private kingdom.
What does it take to activate, motivate and engage?
It takes loss of life, liberty or loved ones to become
enraged.

Instead of ruled by government induced fright.
So before I get back in today's fight
I ease my pain by having hot Epsom soak...
And muse to myself, there's nought as funny as folk!

#WTU #notinthepublicinterest

LOST BROTHER

In Memory of Phil James who lost his fight
January 5th 2020
How heartbreaking.
Today Phil should be waking
To birthday celebrations
Instead of family commiserations
What a grievous crime
For such a length of time
Government have know for years
Despite promoting false fears
THC causes cancer cell apostasis
And maintains homeostasis
Ensuring a state of well-being and good health
But they lie and deceive to improve their wealth
Despite their many a cannabis patent
Their lies and duplicity is becoming blatant
Denying lawful access to ancient herbal remedy
Making now fatal a treatable malady
Leaving our loved ones to die unnecessarily
One might think it was done deliberately
Is it not time we stand as one?
For truth, justice and freedom.
Instead of the rule of law to keep order to maintain
profits?
My deepest empathy and condolences to your family
Send with deepest love from your CannaFam
I mourned your passing brother you were a true
gentleman and kind soul who was failed by a dishonest
government.
You died in vain
Causing such pain
They should be held to account
Its murder almost tantamount

FAREWELL 2019

I bid farewell to 2019
With it goes many a dream
I sit here reflecting on what I have learned
Of new friendships forged and bridges burned
Mourning lost friends, wife and dreams
Realising life's rarely what it seems
Remaining grateful for my home and children
Regardless of the pain and physical burden
Re-evaluating my life and future ambition
Becoming single disabled dad
Is a monumental mission
I have always had a survivor's mentality
So I smile in the face of adversity

FAREWELL OL' CHRISTMAS TREE

Oh Christmas Tree,
Oh Christmas Tree...
It gave me quite a start
Well and Truly saddened my heart
That Millions of you are chopped every year
Without even the shed of a single tear
You're now no longer adorned inside
But Abandoned relics of Yuletide
Lying in gutters or on the drive
Cast aside so businesses can thrive
I truly love you O' Christmas Tree
But better alive than dead for me
They really could save themselves quite a few pound
If they nurtured you in the garden all year round
To bring in to decorate with all festivity Maybe starting
Christmas sustainability?
Oh Why not buy a potted living Christmas tree?

Photo by Alun Buffry

SKETCHES

By

JACQUI MALKIN

Jacqui discovered she could draw when awarded art prize at school. She attended Blackpool college of technology and art (pre diploma),Norwich school of art (graphic design) and worked in a design studio as junior general artist. Jacqui painted on cars and coaches, leather goods for fairs, tattoo designs and sold, bartered and gave away her stuff! Jacqui volunteered as art tutor. She did a degree in multimedia that she says was a waste of time, as computer technology changed too fast but learnt Photoshop. She was inspired by American comics, Beardsley, pre-Raphaelites amongst others.

153

157

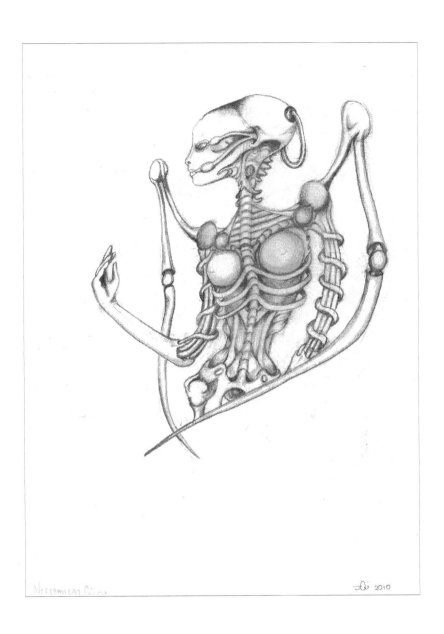

Necronomicon ...   2010

160

161

164

165

169

170

WORDS
BY
STEVE COOK

Steve, son of a Norfolk farming family, has travelled the world. He is a graduate from Norwich Arts School, a poet, artist, photographer, mechanic and inventor. He has previously authored several books of poetry in the "Natural Allies" series and contributed to "Inside My Hat and Other Heads".

DUSK TO DAWN

From out of the mist comes the nightjars' churring
call,
Within, like a mystique, swooping to and fro, out
from where the trees stand tall,
Over the meadows to where the watery air's slow to
warm
The woody oaks along the edge,
Or to the establishing of it's precincts, away from the
North Winds.
As she begins her flight to feed the owlets all;
In the quiet farmyard grain store, the mice; a flutter
stills their struggle.
An anodyne to obvious aid, comes in colours of stony
black
In lesser forms the rooks call, which wield, they
happily thread
The sensitive flight-feathers that give to flap
Where their Autumn lands are still suited to a Ladies
Smock.
Throughout sunlit spells, the ravens will strut to and
fro, their raucous call,
Or like a climax species, a rook for stony flints to
seek a haven
The wisdom of which is coy; and for your attention's
a raving.
Similarly the mountain ash will colonise a gentle
scree or sheltered corrie,
Enough shelter for the lowland birch, a blackbird
comes along.

For the blackbirds everywhere can dwell, in hamlets
or just a kirk,
As long as every day food does abound throughout
the year.
But where the birds on salt-marsh flats, their warm-
blooded sense
Sends us wondering from where; and how they come
and hence
Their mating plumage shows a more spectacular
scene,
for nature in its balance is such a wonderful theme
Which keeps our dreams down a rivulet, rushing over
shallow reefs.
The shell-drake on crustaceans feed, poking about
upon the shelly shore.
The nearby copse of trees and meandering breeze
And all is once again the nightjars' hunting ground,
A tonal measure, searching in the melancholia, way
beyond,
Which we with adjustments to, and not against,
The beautiful harmony around,
That we in our existence mayn't feel so very much
alone,
The dawn of nature's harmonious peace.

TIME TO TURN THE TIDE

Time to turn the tide and rejuvenate oceans
worldwide
Arrived in a maelstrom of cider and fun
But returns seven thirty, up early to run
down to the holy town for a tune up and busk
Hoping quite quietly for a blade of tusk,
Sort the chafe out from the husk,
Equality unity is only a small ask,
A balanced approach to a neighbourly task.
Up early with cheeses and coffee, not in a flask.
Venus shone and The Plough and the great Orion
Distance check, calendula eye bright and byroni
The first morning is cool and bright
And slumbers refreshed all through the night,
A world to greet the friends of light,
An impression to last holding on fast,
An approach of shared stories and fate,
Time to turn the tide if it's coming,
Before it's too late

STAYING SINGLE

Do I love her?
Deep down?
Are we gonna meet,
Now I am in town?
Just an hour.
Sight seeing,
Our love renewing,
Or am I dreaming
Of sweetness and change?
Shooting stars they rearrange,
Sending stardust onto our brains,
In our hair a tingle,
And she appears, from out of the crowd,
Where with guitar playing,
Did mingle – just single.

INTERSTELLA

If I could explain
I've tried to display
The brighter side of my day.
I really have genuine good Karma.
The time I've spent professing good intention,
Supplemented by the odd good invention,
Which is a contribution to a solution
Needed at any expense, life will assert
Bring needed moisture, Mother Nature to convert,
Life to breath in grace to impart
Our visions captured naturally by our heart,
Rounding a curve of time torn struggling,
Emphasis on assisting people's life juggling.
Try to embrace an honest tract,
Our empathy and solace largely in tact,
Verging on sympathies, one singularity packed,
Upon a journey, a path carefully edging along,
Putting ones foot when its standing and strong,
Like a crystal structure honed and out,
Painstakingly looking for highlights to surface in the
prism,
Cooling in a wind of perspiration and love,
Knowing oneself problems to rise above.

ISBN 9781916310704

179

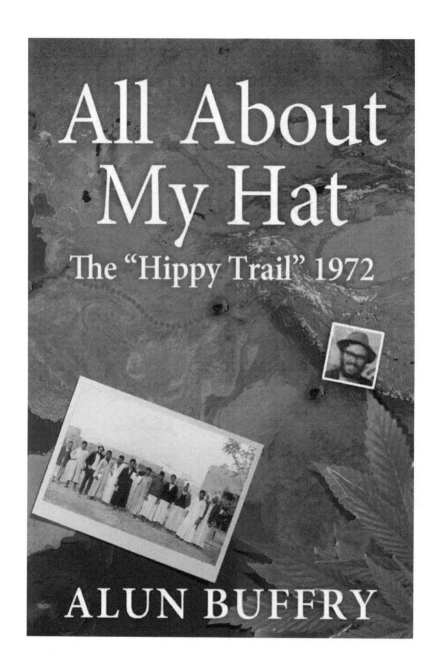

All About My Hat

My Hat

The "Hippy Trail" 1972

ALUN BUFFRY

ISBN 9780993210716

180

ISBN 9780993210778

181

TIME FOR
CANNABIS
The Prison Years
1991 to 1995

Alun Buffry

ISBN 9780993210761

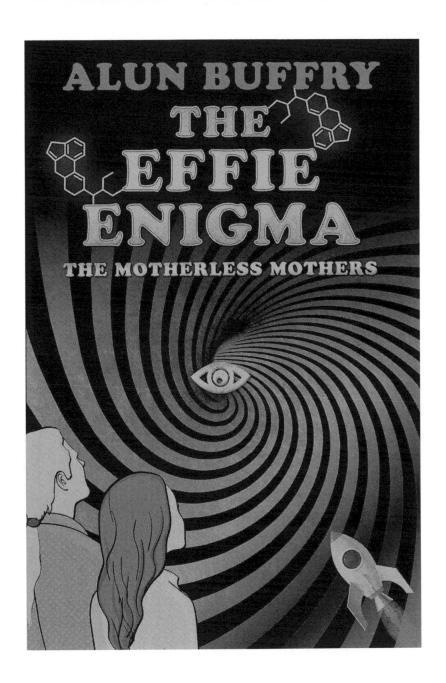

ISBN 9780993210792

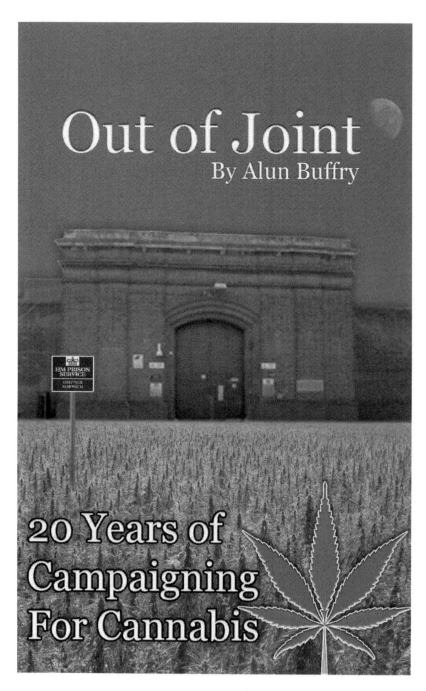

Out of Joint

By Alun Buffry

20 Years of Campaigning For Cannabis

ISBN 9781508420217

ALUN BUFFRY, WILLIAM D HUTCHINSON

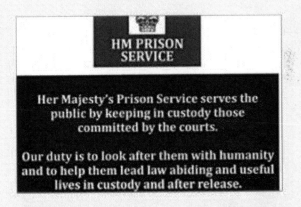

Damage and Humanity in Custody

A Comparison of UK
Prison Regimes by Inmates

ISBN 9781533026224

Fragments
Of
Her Story

Melissa Doordaughter

ISBN 9780993210785

186

Rocky van de Benderskum

What's in a Benderskum?

some stuff I think about dotted with scribbles minus colour

ISBN 9798616877383

We The Undersigned Have a Human Sovereign Right to Cannabis:

Mission Statement

"The acts of possessing, consuming, preparing or cultivating both high or low THC varieties of cannabis at home for personal use causes no significant harm to individuals or others.

People who carry out such activities, causing no harm to others, in the privacy of their own homes, should not live in fear of suffering the harms of criminalisation, as a result of UK drug policy.

WTU therefore declare UK drug policy, in relation to the use, possession, cultivation, preparation and sharing of cannabis for private, adult purposes, to be incompatible with the rights to a freedom of consciousness, private life, beliefs and practices, as defined in the Human Rights Act."

https://www.wtuhq.org/
http://www.ccguide.org/index.php